The DYNAMICS of PERSONAL EFFICIENCY

The DYNAMICS of PERSONAL EFFICIENCY

GUIDES FOR THE FULLER USE OF YOUR CAPACITIES

DONALD A. LAIRD
and
ELEANOR C. LAIRD

HARPER & BROTHERS, PUBLISHERS
New York

THE DYNAMICS OF PERSONAL EFFICIENCY

Printed in the United States of America

FIRST EDITION

Library of Congress catalog card number: 61–12229

Contents

Preface

The Dynamics of Personal Efficiency supplements, but does not take the place of, our older book *Increasing Personal Efficiency,* which was written in 1923 when the "efficiency movement" was in its vigorous adolescence. The older book was unusual in two respects. (1) It was written for the individual who wished to be more efficient in his own life and work rather than for the professional "efficiency expert." (2) It drew material from psychology and physiology, fields that tended to be overlooked by the efficiency or systems engineers who leaned more on accounting, mechanical engineering, and common sense.

The older book was thus somewhat of a hybrid, and its long life suggests that it has some hybrid vigor. It has been selling for more than a third of a century, has been revised four times, and has been translated into Burmese, German, Portuguese, and Swedish.

In recent years many findings that are significant for personal efficiency have been made in such rapidly developing fields as psychoacoustics, biodynamics, and homokinetics. The time has come to report some of these technical findings in nontechnical language, illustrating them with everyday situations the general reader can grasp and apply. The older book would become too large, and its nature changed, if these were simply added to it. Hence this new book.

This book follows the general plan and hybrid contents of the older time-proven edition. The primary emphasis remains on the individual and what he can do to improve his own efficiency, with a secondary emphasis on what he can do to improve the efficiency of those who work for him. Examples are used to demonstrate applications of the principles in housework and personal chores as well as in factories and offices. Photographs, drawings, and charts are included to help the reader grasp the principles and visualize their applications. More space is given to the organization of one's life on an efficient basis than to time-saving gadgets or energy-saving conveniences. Throughout we have been mindful of the young person who is preparing himself to tackle life and of those who are striving to get ahead in the competitive world of white-collar organization men and women.

Most of the living researchers mentioned in the book have given generous assistance in checking the accuracy of the simplified accounts we have written of their findings. Our gratitude for their help is deep and sincere. We are also indebted to the Frank B. Gilbreth Collection in the Purdue University libraries.

DONALD A. LAIRD
ELEANOR C. LAIRD

1. It's Smart To Be Efficient

WOULD YOU LIKE TO GET MORE THINGS DONE, WITH LESS EFFORT and fewer tired feelings? Then increase your personal efficiency. You do not need to buy gadgets and conveniences to make a big gain in efficiency, although they can help. This book will emphasize, instead, proven ways to make fuller use of your capacities so that more is accomplished.

It is easy to become more efficient in every aspect of daily living, from morning dressing, through the day's working time and play periods, to sleeping more efficiently at night. Even children have become more efficient.

Three things are needed:

A strong desire to make fuller use of your capabilities.
A working acquaintance with some principles of efficiency.
The self-management to apply them in your own life and work.

For a start let us see how those work out in modern business. Factory and office executives have a strong desire to operate their firms efficiently, although their desire to be efficient themselves may not be so keen. They have to operate the business efficiently, however, in order to meet competition and stay in business. So they are continually looking for and trying out ways to improve the firm's efficiency, and they are always looking for efficiency-minded employees.

As a result the average factory in the United States has increased its over-all efficiency (productivity per man-hour worked) by from 2 per cent to 6 per cent each year since early this century. That is the average; half the factories did not do so well; some of them lost greatly in efficiency. Each year there are some ten thousand firms that fail and have to go out of business; most of these failures are small concerns that were started by inexperienced men who probably thought it was simple to run a business, but they did not know how to do it efficiently.

It was easy to improve a firm's efficiency at the start of the century when employers in general were not efficiency minded. Today it requires more thought and scientific information. The larger, and more successful, firms have special departments that work solely on methods to improve efficiency. Colleges now have courses to train men and women for this work, not only for business but also for the home and on the farm. There are also associations, such as the Society for the Advancement of Management, in which specialists in efficiency from all over the world share their experiences and improve their own job efficiency.

The special departments that plan, test, and install methods that will increase efficiency are usually called Methods, or Planning, or Industrial Engineering. They may recommend costly but labor-saving new machinery, or a better procedure for a seemingly simple job, such as a more efficient way to use vacuum cleaners, which we will describe in a moment.

II

The yearly gains in factory and office efficiency are small in comparison with the gains the individual could make for himself. There are two reasons for that.

1. Most people have paid no attention to being more efficient in their personal lives. William James, Harvard's first professor of psychology, wrote: "Men habitually use only a small part of the powers they actually possess." John Wanamaker, the poor-born ruddy-faced six-footer who became a merchant prince, said: "Hardly any businessman is half what he might be." And Dr. Arthur G. Bills, author of *The Psychology of Efficiency,* told his students: "Most of the things

we do in a day's work are performed with one-fourth to one-half of the efficiency we might use."

More people need a strong desire to make fuller use of their capacities, to work out better methods for themselves to use.

2. Most people are not acquainted with the techniques researchers have discovered which enable people to get more done with less effort. These researches provide some principles of general usefulness, and take much of the guesswork out of efficiency. For example:

Inefficient Zigzag method — Efficient Hairpin Looping method

1. EFFICIENCY IN VACUUM CLEANING

Two methods of using the vacuum cleaner wand. The lines show the course of the middle of the nozzle across the floor. The text explains why one method is more efficient. (Adapted from Dr. Ralph M. Barnes)

Looping or curving movements can be made more efficiently than back-and-forth zigzags. Spencerian handwriting is looping. When this principle is applied to vacuuming as shown in the drawing, there is a 15 per cent saving in the time needed to vacuum a room.

People do not read so well as they could. Most adults can read half again as rapidly as they do, and get twice as much meaning from what they read, if they

Do not move lips or pronounce the words.
Read entire phrases rather than words or letter by letter.
Read to get the meanings.
Keep practicing to get more meanings per minute.

People forget errands and instructions and names and faces they could remember if they would

Simply try to remember the item accurately at the time it occurs, when it is read, or when you are told it.
Think about it actively at the time it occurs.
Refresh your memory of the item several times the same day.

People lose time and tempers hunting for articles they have misplaced because they do not follow consistently an efficient system for putting things away in the right places.

They use more energy than necessary because they do not know how to use muscles efficiently, and have not organized their tasks to eliminate useless motions.

They have trouble concentrating on their work when they could cut down many of the distractions in their environment and in addition use methods to help them concentrate under distracting conditions.

All in all, a little reading can give the average person ideas which can improve his personal efficiency in dozens of ways—if he uses self-management to apply them in his own life and work.

III

Increasing one's personal efficiency does not require harder work, or longer, or no resting, or no play. Quite the contrary. The efficient way is almost always the easier way, but easy does not mean doing nothing. We still need a will to work, however.

It is a basic principle that efficiency makes a task easier, reduces annoyances and distractions, and makes the work more interesting and comfortable. That is the approach of the National Institute of Industrial Psychology, which was started in England in 1918, and which has helped to bring about amazing increases in productivity.

For example, girls doing the easy but monotonous work of folding handkerchiefs all day long found their output doubled when they were made to rest briefly six times an hour and their work was arranged so that they could either sit or stand while doing it. Resting is needed, even for light tasks. And changes of work posture—either sit or stand at the work—are also needed.

Another example: Miners who were doing the heavy work of loosening coal from the seam saw their output increase 16 per cent after they had been taught an easier way to swing their picks. They had been swinging in a zigzag fashion, and tiring themselves out by checking the pick as it bounced away from the hard surface. They were taught to use a looping stroke, in a slow-and-easy rhythm, relaxing on the upward part of the stroke, instead of whamming away by brute force. Frantic exertion is never so efficient as steadily-paced exertion, especially when there is a brief relaxing, however short, between exertions.

Unless it is an easier way, it is not likely to be more efficient. And almost always there is an easier way, or some short cut that is worth finding.

IV

To the engineer efficiency means how much energy a machine can turn out in proportion to the energy it uses. Steam engines have an efficiency of that sort of about 15 per cent when kept in good operating condition; for every 100 calories of fuel the engine uses it turns

Pulling least efficient

Pushing most efficient

But this man is pushing inefficiently, as the next illustration shows

2. MORE EFFICIENT TO PUSH THAN TO PULL

out only 15 calories of work done—most of the energy put in does no useful work. Automobile engines may go as high as 25 per cent in efficiency when well tuned. Diesel engines are usually more efficient than either, reaching as high as 35 per cent.

How about human efficiency on this basis? People can be—but seldom are—more efficient than even a diesel engine. The trained athlete has a muscular efficiency of more than 40 per cent. But the usual sedentary person has a muscular efficiency of around 20 to 30 per cent, about that of his automobile engine.

Muscular efficiency is influenced not only by how sedentary the person has been, but also by the work methods he uses. Pushing a wheelbarrow, for example, requires fewer calories to move the same load than pulling it. Push instead of pull, and usually you will have higher muscular efficiency.

Efficiency in walking depends partly upon the speed at which you walk. A slow walk is the least efficient, a rapid walk a little more efficient. The most efficient speed for the average man is three to three and one-half miles an hour, a bit more rapid than most people do walk. The most efficient walking speed for women, is a little slower than for men; this is because women have shorter legs.

When you are in a hurry, would it be more efficient to walk as rapidly as possible, or to run slowly? About the fastest you can walk is five and one-half miles an hour. This is also the speed of slow running. Metabolism tests show that a slow run is more efficient; it

Efficient
—pushing at center of weight
—pushing mostly with legs and shoulders

Inefficient
—pushing too high up
—pushing with back and arms

3. THE EFFICIENT WAY TO PUSH

uses fewer calories to cover the same distance as a rapid walk. The gait used in slow running gives the body a forward thrust, or momentum, which makes the body partly self-propelling, and once under way less energy is needed to keep going.

V

For many of the important things we do, however, there is no way to measure either the calories of energy put into it or the energy value of the work turned out. How would you determine the energy value of being able to work amidst distracting noises? Or of being able to work with less eye strain?

In such instances we have to be guided mostly by the end results. When learning to typewrite by the touch system, for instance, Dr. Gary C. Myers found that the typists gained most speed when accuracy was emphasized from the beginning. So we conclude it is more efficient to learn touch typing by striving for accuracy rather than for speed as such, although we do not know about the calories of energy involved. That "accuracy principle" applies to most things we do and can be used as a *guide* for increasing personal efficiency: we come out ahead in the long run by working accurately rather than hastily. *

As another illustration, suppose you want to remember some information to present at a meeting tomorrow afternoon. Would it be more efficient to memorize it the first thing when you get up in the morning, or should you wait until you have been up a couple hours? Tests by Dr. Philip Worchel have shown that people remember more of what they memorize after they have been up an hour or two and have become fully awake and reactive. Another example of gauging efficiency by the end results.

Efficiency can also be estimated by the length of time it takes to accomplish the same end results. Consider setting a dining-room table, where the end results are about the same whichever way it is done. It takes much less time if a wheeled tray is used to take most of the things to the table in one trip rather than many trips with a handful at a time. When tests were made of this in a Vermont kitchen, a wheeled tray saved 389 steps a day. This illustrates the "carry-all principle," which is widely used in factories, and is a useful *guide* for individuals to follow. Why make several trips when you could do it in one, if you planned ahead? *

Saving effort is another aspect of efficiency. This is not the kind that is shown by the calories of energy used. This effort is the feeling of discomfort, or reluctance, over having to do something; of having to force yourself; or of having no will for the particular work. You feel this effort when trying to read in a dim light, or when having to do something you dislike doing, or which you do not think is important to do. One housewife dislikes dusting, and it takes more effort of this sort for her to do it than it does to scrub the floor, which she enjoys, but which uses two to three times as many calories as the dusting.

People who do light but monotonous work feel this effort when they say: "I'm not tired, but I am tired of doing this." The girls who were folding handkerchiefs felt that effort, but it was cut down and they zoomed in efficiency when they were given many short breaks and changes of position every hour.

This feeling of effort becomes almost overpowering toward the end of a long coffee break. Dr. Arthur G. Bills checked some people who

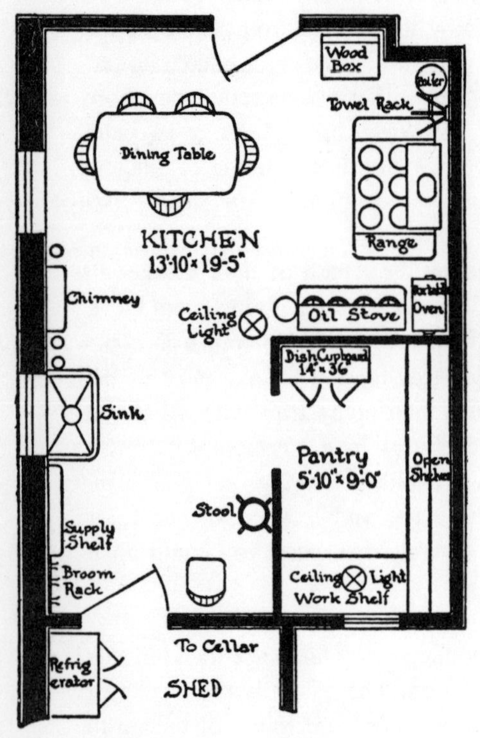

4. THE ORIGINAL FARMHOUSE KITCHEN

There are many suggestions for the betterment of the workplace of the home in these two kitchens. The second plan brought about a saving of 1 hour and 40 minutes in the time spent in kitchen work each day. Here are the stages by which this tremendous saving was accomplished.

had been doing mental work which was difficult but did not require many calories of energy. After the first two minutes of the rest pause they felt strongly reluctant about going back to their work. It would have taken a great deal of effort to resume work then. But their desire to get back to work increased steadily to reach its highest point after they had rested seven minutes.

From then on their interest in returning to work nose-dived. After ten minutes' rest they felt less like resuming work than they had after only two minutes' rest. And after seventeen minutes' rest they had to use all the effort they could muster to go back. For that job a seven-minute rest period was more efficient than a seventeen-minute one.

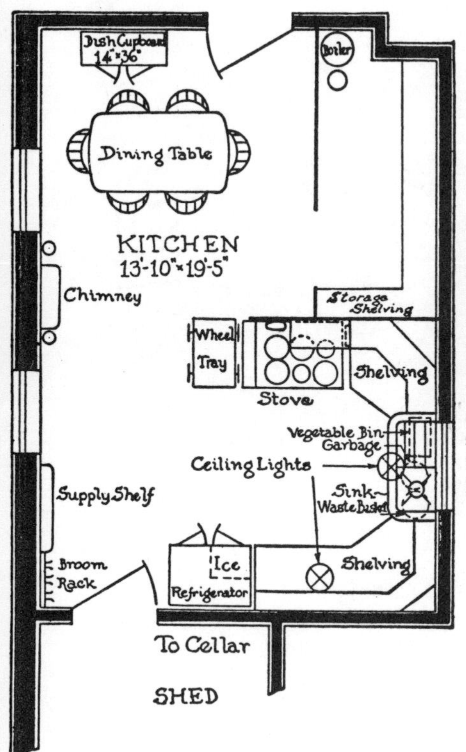

5. HOW THE KITCHEN WAS CHANGED

Adding a stack table saved 139 steps. Putting a drain board at the sink saved 234 more steps. Adopting a wheel tray to transport things from one place to another in more than handful lots saved 389 more steps. Rearranging the utensils saved another 168 steps. Rearranging the supply of foods saved 218. Making the whole layout more compact saved 154 steps. An electric mixer saved 9 steps. (Courtesy Vermont Agricultural Experiment Station; work of Marianne Muse)

There is the least feeling of effort, and usually better quality of work, and more end results, if the individual finds the work interesting, or thinks it is important. Then he has some natural enthusiasm for the work instead of an "Oh! hum" attitude toward it. More will-to-work, which is one of the most important factors in personal efficiency.

It's smart to be interested in what you have to do. Tests show that merely pretending interest helps, although it is not so efficiency-helping as the genuine article.

And it's smart to be efficiency-minded in every way. To be on the lookout for, and trying out easier, more comfortable, more satisfying ways of doing things. Then make a habit of doing them in those more efficient ways.

6. MAKE YOUR WORK IMPORTANT

Personal efficiency is usually higher and the will-to-work stronger when the person feels that his work is important. (From the booklet "The Worry-Go-Round" courtesy The Connecticut Mutual Life Insurance Company)

There is a wonderland of better ways to help you accomplish more with less effort and to make better use of your capacities. Many of the ways are obvious, once they are called to your attention, as in the account underneath the drawings of the farmhouse kitchen. Others are not so obvious, and require fuller explanations.

Some of the ways depend upon improvements in the environment and working arrangements, as in that kitchen. Others—and more likely to be overlooked—depend upon making more efficient use of one's capacities; such as emphasizing accuracy when learning touch typing, or using muscles better as with those miners.

We will take you through this wonderland, reporting efficiency-increasing methods and techniques which are based on experimental research, or on accepted scientific principles, or on practical experience. Special emphasis will be given to ways that will be useful in organizing your own life, not only as a worker but also as student, housewife, or self-employed professional person; not only in factory or office but also at home.

This wonderland will not help you much, however, unless you have a deep desire to increase your efficiency and have a will-to-work. So we are going to become better acquainted with three famous efficiency-minded men, thus hoping to sharpen your desire to increase your personal efficiency.

2. How Thomas Jefferson Increased His Efficiency

I

WHY ARE SOME PEOPLE MUCH MORE EFFICIENT THAN OTHERS?

A few people are accused, somewhat in jest, of looking for short cuts because they are lazy. A seventeen-year-old student in an eastern college was called lazy by his fraternity brothers because he nailed his bedroom slippers to the wall, letting the nails hold his feet up for him while he studied! At least he studied, which was more than some of his tormentors did. It was the one who was "too lazy to hold his own feet up" who became Chief Justice Holmes of the United States Supreme Court.

But there is more to personal efficiency than short cuts and easier ways to get a task done. Personal efficiency has the broader goal of helping the individual make fuller use of his capacities. Not merely time-saving gadgets, but also one's life plan.

The person with a strong desire to be personally efficient is far from lazy, regardless of how his short cutting impresses onlookers. He works hard, though efficiently, to do the things that will count in his self-development and advancement. He tries in all ways to live efficiently so he can work more efficiently; he leaves parties early so he will be rested for tomorrow, for instance.

As he organizes his life on an efficiency basis he is likely to be more interested in building his future than pleased with his past accomplishments. He is not a self-satisfied egoist, nor a gloomy failure who is afraid to try different ways. Rather, he is usually spurred on by a healthy amount of dissatisfaction. As Dean Stanley F. Teele, of Harvard's Graduate School of Business told the members of the American Management Association, "Dissatisfaction with oneself, with one's performance, is an essential for improvement."

Such motivation was interestingly shown by the man who was the first to stimulate Americans toward becoming the most efficiency-minded people on earth. He used all sorts of efficiency gadgets and short cuts, but, also organized his life so he could make fuller use of his capacities in directions that counted.

II

Thomas Jefferson intentionally organized his life so he would be more efficient, and was so pleased with the results that he became the world's first Ambassador of Efficiency. He was probably the most efficiency-minded person of his time, more so than even Benjamin Franklin.

Jefferson had some pressing need for thinking about efficiency because he operated a 5,000-acre plantation at Monticello. There were some two hundred workers who raised crops on a large scale, and ran the many small industries that were needed to supply the large establishment—a brick kiln, textile manufacture, sawmill, cabinet-making, ironworking, grist and flour mill, harnessmaking shop, and an experimental garden and nursery. (With present-day farm machinery, 25 men can farm 5,000 acres. Machinery has become more efficient since Jefferson's day. Have people?)

What made Jefferson more interested in efficiency than other Virginia planters, some of whom had even larger establishments?

III

Jefferson's consuming interest in efficiency blossomed after his first year at college, and was directed toward organizing his own life rather than the plantation. When he was a sandy-haired freckled boy of fourteen his father died, leaving him considerable wealth and a mentally defective brother. The next year young Jefferson, with no thought of efficiency or any goal in particular in his head, took his violin and went to William and Mary College.

The six-foot-two-inch shy country youth was overwhelmed by what struck him as a large metropolis. Williamsburg's population was then only about one thousand, but it was a city in comparison with his isolated rural home and was moreover well supplied with facilities for worldly pleasures.

Jefferson's voice was too much of a monotone for him to join in the singing at the taverns, but he played his violin vigorously to help the merriment along. His first year at college was literally fiddled away, and his teachers probably saw little future for this gangling under-achiever from the back country.

But during that first summer vacation he took stock of himself and his future and reached some decisions about making fuller use of whatever worth-while talents he might have. He decided to be more efficient personally, something many people delay until much later in life.

When he returned to classes that autumn he took along his inseparable violin but left fiddling behind him forever. He had resolved to manage himself, to strive for long-range goals, and not follow the temptations of the moment. The loafing, fiddling, and gambling during his first year had seemed pleasant at the time, but as he considered his future that summer he judged his first college year as a lost year.

Now he *budgeted his time*, so he would be less likely to skimp on those activities that would count in preparing for his future. He would henceforth invest his time, not merely spend it—a good start toward improving one's personal efficiency. A self-made time schedule gives the right of way for activities that count. It helps one keep on the main track, avoid aimless detours.

He had also resolved to *get up early*, another good start—provided the person goes to bed early enough to have sufficient sleep. And provided the morning hours thus gained are devoted to making headway, as "Long Tom" Jefferson's were from then on.

Some days he worked more than fifteen hours, making up for the previous year's lost time. He became an achiever. That long, long workday may be a good start toward increasing personal efficiency, or it may be a trap. Sagaciously placed *rest periods* are essential if it is not to be a trap. Jefferson got those through his violin. When it became difficult to concentrate or remember, he would play "Thou Soft Flowing Avon," selections from Handel, Corelli, or his other favorites. Then he would turn back to the main track, refreshed, although he may have wanted to keep on playing.

7. PLAN IT YOURSELF

There is usually more interest in personal efficiency, and the will-to-work is stronger when the person is working on something he planned himself. (From the booklet "Satisfaction Guaranteed;" courtesy The Connecticut Mutual Life Insurance Company)

He also began to *use idle moments* while traveling or waiting to make further headway. Later he designed a portable writing desk, about the size of an elongated brief case, so he could keep busy while traveling. He wrote the Declaration of Independence on this; today thousands of people look at this desk in the Smithsonian Institution in Washington.

Years later he wrote a friend, "It is wonderful how much can be done if we are always doing." His quest for personal efficiency extended in many other directions than time budgeting, early rising, rest pauses, and always doing things that helped him make headway.

IV

From that fateful summer of decision on, for sixty-seven accomplishment-filled years, Jefferson not only was always doing but also testing out and adopting better ways for doing.

8. JEFFERSON USED SPARE MOMENTS

Jefferson designed this portable desk for use while traveling and wrote the Declaration of Independence on it. He worked with this desk on his lap, on a table, or on a chair, the adjustable tilt top of the desk providing an efficient writing or reading angle. The drawer containing writing materials opened conveniently at the end of the desk. (Courtesy The Smithsonian Institution)

There was his favorite work chair, for example, which would turn so he would not twist his back when reaching for things at one side or the other. Swivel chairs were unknown until he designed this one to help his efficiency.

He also wanted a more efficient desk, so he designed one that could be pulled up to that swivel chair. The desk top could be quickly tilted to one angle for reading, another for writing, another for drawing building plans. A drawer at one end held his writing and drawing supplies and could be left open without interfering with his elbows; he did not have to hunt for his writing tools and did not worry about knocking them off the desk top. Swivel chair and desk were made, of course, in his own cabinet shop, and Jefferson likely helped in their construction. (When he moved to the White House he took along his personal set of cabinet tools and his violin.)

On his walks around the plantation and industries he carried a walking stick he had devised to make it easier to sit and rest. This was in effect three sticks in one, pivoted together. The three could be spread out to form a tripod with a canvas seat (made in his textile shop) on top. A convenient place to sit while he watched work and pondered how a task could be made easier. The many hunters, campers, and race fans who use sitting sticks today may not be aware of their debt to efficiency-minded Jefferson.

Perched on his sitting stick, Jefferson watched workmen plowing and noticed that the rich clay stuck to the plow and slowed work. Farmers had always struggled through clay and complained about the lost time but never did anything about it. But efficiency-minded Jefferson designed various plowshares until he produced one that would turn sticky soil and keep as clean as a hound's tooth. Plowing was made easier, quicker, more efficient.

V

This plow illustrates a characteristic which makes Jefferson noteworthy—he tried to get others to be efficiency-minded. He can be fairly called the first salesman and Ambassador of Efficiency.

Samples of his new plowshare were passed along to others to copy. The French government awarded him a special gold medal for the benefit it brought to French farmers. He patented none of his numerous efficiency-increasing inventions, but was always promoting them and encouraging others all over the world to use them and become more efficient.

Another example is the way he helped others make copies of their important letters. Copies were usually boresomely made by hand. Jefferson tried out inks that would give a fair facsimile copy when a blank sheet of paper was pressed on the freshly written letter before the ink had dried. More successful was the polygraph, which had just been invented by someone else. This consisted of two pens connected so that when the master pen moved, the slave pen moved in exactly the same patterns. Simply place a sheet of paper under each pen, write with one pen, and the other makes a copy.

Jefferson was enthusiastic about the polygraph. Being efficiency-minded, he devised several improvements in it which the inventor was grateful to have. And always the Ambassador of Efficiency, Jefferson urged his friends to use the new device, sending them polygraph copies rather than the original of his letters to demonstrate what it would do.

When he became acquainted with how Eli Whitney was manufacturing guns with interchangeable parts, Jefferson immediately saw the possibilities of this mass-production method for increasing the efficiency of the nation's beginning industries. Jefferson became a self-appointed promoter of similar mass production for other articles. Many of the 1,200 letters he wrote in his own hand during a typical year—aided by polygraph copies—were long explanations of this new mass-production method and urging its adoption in general.

No other person of his time did as much to spread the idea of increasing efficiency. Jefferson was respected and influential, and his urgings were taken seriously. He must be given credit for starting the ground swell that made America the most efficiency-minded continent on earth. But many people still have not caught the message as they plod along at a low level of personal efficiency.

VI

Although Jefferson was occupied by many other affairs and worked only part time on questions of efficiency, he was such a confirmed "efficiency addict" and persistent Ambassador of Efficiency that he gave many others an impetus to take up the same addiction.

But he was a little ahead of his times in this, and there was no one to take his place as efficiency advocate. It was not until the beginning of the present century that the times were right and two men came on the scene and separately devoted their full time to creative experimentation on improving efficiency.

These men were Frederick W. Taylor and Frank B. Gilbreth. The brilliance of their work and the vigor with which they spread the messages of efficiency got the efficiency movement under way in earnest. A new era began in factories and offices, and spread later to farms and homes.

But let's give "Long Tom" and the resolutions he made that summer the glory for preparing the ground for the few thousand full-time planning, methods, industrial engineering, and efficiency specialists in today's factories and offices. And the story of efficiency-minded Jefferson may give the reader the little push he needs to devote himself more enthusiastically to increasing his own personal efficiency.

3. Efficient Walking, Running, Stair Climbing, and Wheelbarrowing

I

THOMAS JEFFERSON WAS ONE OF THE FIRST TO TRY TO FIND THE most efficient ways to walk and to use wheelbarrows. Thanks to the automobile, we no longer have to walk as much as in his day. But we still have to walk, and it may be harder now because we have become sedentary and do not walk nearly so efficiently as we might. If a really brisk half-hour walk tires you out, you can profit by applying what Jefferson and his successors learned about walking, running, and stair climbing.

What they have also learned about wheelbarrowing can be applied whenever you have to push, pull, lift, or carry. And despite all the mechanization of jobs, there remains a great deal of work that requires an old-fashioned wheelbarrow and man power. The *U.S. Census of Manufacturers* records that in 1954 nearly a half million wheelbarrows were made. Sad to state, most of that half million were constructed so that they are not nearly so efficient as they should be, as will be clear in a few paragraphs.

II

Jefferson liked to walk: hard walking on rough and hilly ground which would give most moderns sore legs the next day. He made long inspection trips around his 5,000 acres on foot instead of riding horseback as most Virginia planters did. "What are our legs for, if not to walk with?" he said.

With his consuming interest in efficiency it was inevitable that he would try to walk as efficiently as possible. The pedometer had just been invented, and he owned one of the first in America. On his walks he hung the pedometer on his belt, and the jar of each step moved the mechanism ahead one notch, similar to today's self-winding

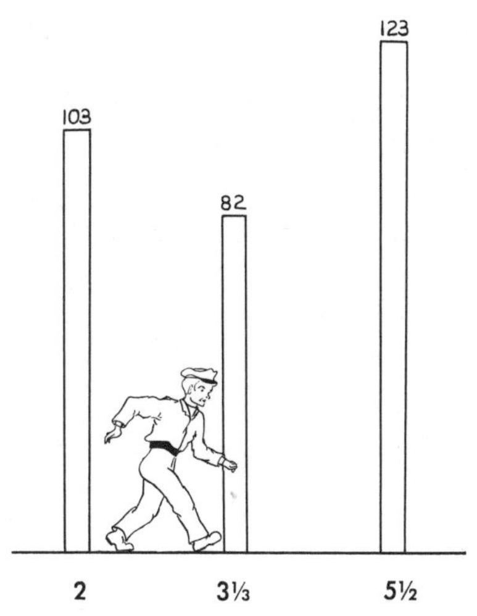

9. CALORIES USED TO WALK ONE MILE

The medium speed was most efficient
Speed in miles per hour
(Data from Drs. F. G. Benedict and H. Murschhauser)

watches. Using this pedometer as an indicator of how far he walked, he came to the conclusion that the most efficient speed was four miles an hour.

More recent tests, in which the calories of energy used when walking on the level and not carrying a load were measured, show clearly that the most efficient speed is from three to three and three-quarter miles an hour. The chart shows how one man used calories while walking at different speeds. He was not sedentary, but in prime physical condition; a sedentary person uses more calories when exercising than does an active person.

For the average woman, who has shorter legs, the most efficient walking speed is around two and one-quarter miles per hour. For Jefferson, who was unusually long-legged, the four miles may have been the most efficient speed.

In terms of steps taken, 100 to 120 steps a minute works out as most efficient for the average person.

Victor Herbert, who habitually walked as rapidly as he could without running—"a man in a hurry"—used an inefficient speed. His jogging walk was probably a good thing for him, however, since it was about the only activity he engaged in that kept him from being completely sedentary.

Here are some other aspects of walking efficiency which modern research has uncovered:

When a load is being carried, the most efficient speed is slower. With a forty-pound load on level ground, the best speed is about two and one-half miles an hour for the average man.

If a heavier load than that is being carried by a man who is used to such carrying, he should rest for about two minutes after walking one-third of a mile. If he is not used to such work, or is sedentary, he should rest after a shorter walk, and take a longer rest.

Running is usually less efficient than walking. About the only exception to this is that the slowest possible running is more efficient than the fastest possible walking, such as Victor Herbert favored.

Walking on a wet or slippery surface is much less efficient. Also more hazardous.

Walking is less efficient on a bumpy surface, such as cobblestones, warped floors, or rough countryside.

III

Physical characteristics make some people considerably less efficient than others when walking. Overweight people are less efficient; they simply have more weight to carry—a forty pound load, perhaps—and should slow down accordingly. Of course they might reduce their weight, too.

Corpulent people and pregnant women are least efficient of all in walking. The corpulency throws their trunk weight off balance and they have to use additional energy to keep from falling forward.

The walking efficiency of a short-legged person is lowered if he uses a stride that is unnaturally long for his build, as often happens when he tries to keep in step with a longer-legged person. Swing your legs in the stride "that comes naturally"; to make extra speed, merely take more steps per minute, not longer ones—speed up, don't stretch.

Sedentariness is especially influential on walking, and not primarily because the leg muscles are flabbier than they should be. All the bodily processes that convert energy into muscular work are at low ebb in the sedentary person. All muscle activity, as well as walking, is affected. He uses more oxygen, gets out of breath sooner, and his heart races more than does the person who is in good condition.

Walking is a good way to start to get out of a sedentary condition. Simply walk a little longer each day, and a little more rapidly, until you can walk briskly for a half-hour and not feel it. This cannot be accomplished in a week; it is more likely to take three or four months of daily walking.

IV

Walking up a grade is less efficient than on the level. A steep walk can quickly exhaust you, unless you are in the pink of condition. Climbing ordinary stairs requires from fifteen to twenty times as many calories as walking on the level. But to climb off a pound of body fat, a one hundred and fifty-pound person would have to climb upstairs about 1,000 times!

Walking down a grade is also less efficient. Going downstairs requires about five times as many calories as walking on the level. In this case the extra energy is expended in "holding back" as we go down grade. It is a fallacy to imagine that gravity does the work for us; we have to hold back firmly against gravity. Incidentally, it is "holding back" that is likely to make the leg muscles sore the next day.

It is less efficient to walk while wearing low-cut oxfords. Shoes that cover the ankles are more efficient; the shoe supports the ankle and foot joints so that calf and foot muscles do not tire so rapidly.

It improves walking efficiency to swing the arms slightly, in rhythm with the stride. Not a wide swing; just enough to maintain the center of gravity of the trunk (weight about seventy-pounds in a one hundred and fifty-pound person) which is thrown slightly off balance on each step.

Walk more on the ball of the foot than on toes or heel, so that the arch of the foot carries the bulk of the weight. If you "pound" when

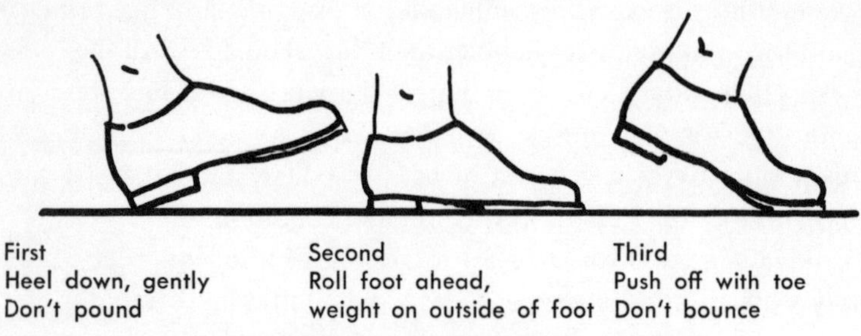

10. EFFICIENT FOOTWORK WHEN WALKING

walking, it is a sign you are putting too much weight on the heel. If you "bounce," you are using the toes too much. Shoes with high heels force one to walk mostly on the toes.

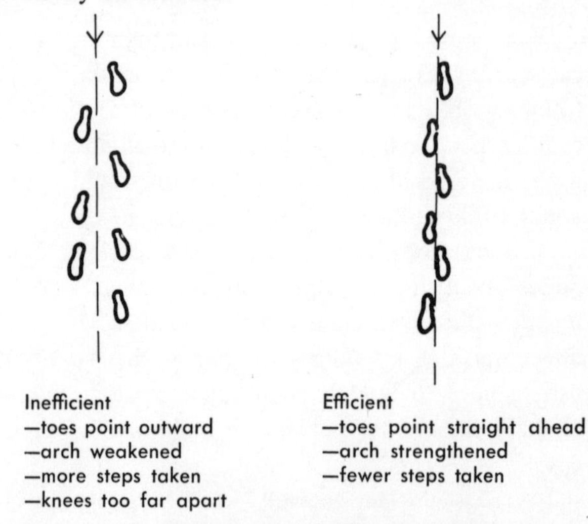

11. TRACKS MADE WHEN WALKING

It is more efficient to walk with the toes pointing almost straight ahead—Indian fashion. If you "waddle," your toes are turned out too much, or are slightly deformed. When the toes are turned outward, the arch of the foot is weakened and in addition you are likely to have a zigzag walk, the legs moving diagonally rather than straight ahead. Toes straight ahead, or even turned slightly inward, make for greatest leverage and most efficient walking. Unfortunately, as one becomes tired there is a tendency to walk with toes out, which makes it even more tiring.

Keep the knees close together when walking, not sprawl-legged, so that the bones of the upper leg are parallel; knees relaxed, not stiff.

Keep the center of gravity of your body over your feet. When starting to walk tilt slightly—only slightly—forward from the ankles. Don't lean forward from your hips, as a gorilla does, or as if you were "looking for pennies" on the sidewalk.

V

There are times when we have to *run*—to catch the bus, for instance—although running is generally less efficient than walking. Perhaps because we run so seldom, we usually do it most inefficiently. Running is not speeded-up walking, but a very different activity, as the following *guides* illustrate.

Warm up before trying to run full tilt. Running makes much greater demands on vital bodily processes. Start out at a slow jog for a minute before increasing your pace.

Take off from your toes, not from the entire foot as in walking.

Land on the ball of your foot, not the heel.

Lean forward a little—only a little—from the hips. The more you lean, the faster you have to run to keep from falling forward.

Keep chest and head up, as if you were leading with your chest; eyes ahead, not on the ground or your feet.

Hold your hands up so your elbows are about at right angles. Keep elbows close to your sides, clenched fists pointing straight ahead. Don't wave to the bus driver.

Swing arms slightly forward and backward—not diagonally—in rhythm with your pace. Don't swing your shoulders.

Knees should be raised a little higher than when walking; only a little. As in walking, keep knees and ankles flexible to absorb the shocks.

Swing your legs from the hip joint mostly. This gives a longer stride and greater muscle power.

Abdomen should be held taut to protect your insides from the jarring.

Contrary to some popular beliefs, there is no harm in women running while they are menstruating; jumping, however, may not be desirable.

VI

Stair climbing requires many times as much energy as walking or running. It is also different in the following points:

About fifty steps a minute is most efficient; this is about half as many as when walking.

12. EFFICIENT STAIR CLIMBING
—Lean forward slightly
—Climbing foot firmly on step
—Start slowly

Put the entire foot, not just the ball and toes, on the next step. Put it firmly on the step before raising your body weight.

Put the foot well back on the step, not on the front edge.

Lean slightly forward from the ankles up, as in walking; not from the hips, as in fast running.

Use the hand rail if you are sedentary. But climb enough that soon you can use no hands and not get out of breath.

Take the first few steps slowly, to give the physiological processes time to shift automatically into higher gear.

Stair climbing is much easier for short-legged people than for the long-legged. It is also easier for the short-legged to lift heavy loads by crouching and then straightening their legs. This is because of the way muscle power is applied to straighten the leg.

The muscle doing most of this work is the big quadriceps extensor located on the front of the thigh. The moving end of this muscle is attached to the lower leg about an inch and a half below the knee joint. The longer the bone below this attachment, the more pull has to be applied to straighten the leg. This lever arrangement is more efficient for speed than for lifting strength, but is the one that has to be used when climbing or lifting.

Women in general have much shorter legs in proportion to their total height. This gives them an advantage for climbing or lifting.

Experienced employment interviewers apply this by giving preference to short, stocky men for work of this sort. The short man can climb a ladder, or walk up a grade, much easier than a tall man of the same weight. But the tall man wins out in walking on the level.

VII

Jefferson, the builder and architect, also had a practical interest in *wheelbarrowing*. Perched on his sitting stick, he watched his workmen move bricks in wheelbarrows. Much of their energy, be observed, went into keeping the load balanced, so he had a two-wheeled barrow built. After this proved much more efficient, Monticello was equipped with two-wheeled barrows.

A century after Jefferson's studies of wheelbarrowing physiologists began to measure the calories of energy used by men working with various barrow arrangements. This gave a more precise indication of the relative efficiency than Jefferson could get. Some of the physiologists' findings showed that:

It takes less human energy—is more efficient—to push a barrow than to pull it. That principle applies in general. When an automobile stalls, push it, don't try to pull it by man power. When moving heavy furniture, push it, don't pull. One exception is a stubborn mule; pull him because he is more likely to kick than bite.

The barrow handles should be higher from the ground for a tall man than for a short man. The right height is about three inches below the fingertips when standing erect between the handles. The handles on conventional barrows are too low for most people.

The principle illustrated by that applies in general. The height of work surfaces should be matched to the individual's build. When the work surface—desk top, kitchen sink, sewing machine, assembly bench—cannot be raised or lowered, a chair or stool that can be adjusted to the person's height should be used. Or the short housewife can have a low platform built to stand on while she is working at the kitchen sink; portable stools can be used for small children to reach the washbowl.

The load on a barrow should be positioned so that it is balanced when you are pushing it. This is seldom possible with conventional

13. SIT AT THE RIGHT HEIGHT

Fitting individual differences to get the most efficient working height with an adjustable utility stool. (Courtesy Fisher Scientific Company)

barrows because the wheel sticks out in front of the load. When a barrow that is designed for efficiency is fully loaded, only about fifteen pounds has to be lifted by the handles to balance the load on the wheel—easy does it.

When a loaded barrow is to be pushed up an incline, it is easier (that is, more efficient) if the load is centered a little nearer the handles. That half million of barrows made per year seem to have been designed to push loads up hills.

The most energy-consuming part of barrow work is the starting and stopping. A stop before reaching the destination is inefficient,

Inefficient
—leaning forward, off balance
—back bent

Efficient
—body balanced over feet
—back erect

14. GET THE HEIGHT RIGHT FOR STANDING

unless it is a long haul and a rest pause en route may add to efficiency. As a general principle, never set a load down to visit, and don't stand

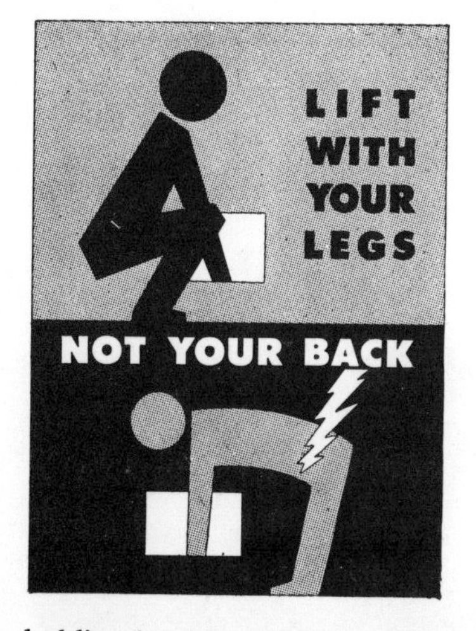

15. LIFT WITH YOUR LEGS
(Courtesy National Safety Council)

holding it while you visit. Hold off the visiting until you have reached the destination and can drop the load.

Barrows with rubber tires are easier to push, especially over rough surfaces. The ancient Egyptians applied that principle in building the pyramids. The large stones were moved on their ancient substitute for rubber tires—pigs' bladders which were filled with water under pressure.

Lift the barrow—or any heavy load—by using the powerful thigh muscles rather than the back muscles. Keep the back erect, vertical, and simply bend the knees—scrooch, they call it in Scotland—until the hands can grasp the handles. Then lift the load by straightening the knees—unscrooching—the way a scissors jack operates. And the fingers will grasp the handles more securely if the hand is bent slightly backward at the wrist.

It is most efficient to push the barrow at a brisk walk—about eighty to ninety steps a minute. As we have seen, a slow walk, or a run, is least efficient. That illustrates another rather general *guide* for efficiency in using muscles: efficiency is lowered if we move too slowly or too rapidly. It's difficult to beat a good, steady pace. Spurt once in a while, or slow down, to break the monotony if you wish, but make a good, steady pace your goal in most muscle activities that last longer than a few minutes.

4. Taylor's Discoveries About Efficiency

I

WE MIGHT NOT HAVE COFFEE BREAKS TODAY IF A CONGRESSIONAL investigation in 1911 had not looked into the efficiency of government arsenals, shipyards, and ordnance plants. This committee gave the world its first glimpse of the behind-the-scenes advances which had recently been made in improving efficiency. The view amazed everyone except a few insiders. Oddly enough, the star witness, the man responsible, did not drink coffee—he did not enjoy it.

Blunt-talking, determined, wealthy, but plainly dressed Frederick W. Taylor was the star witness who amazed the congressmen and the public. A handful of business leaders had known about his accomplishments, but until this investigation neither lawmakers nor the public realized how inefficiently most businesses—and individuals—operated.

The skeptical congressmen could scarcely believe that Taylor had found ways to shorten the workday, give workers rest pauses, and yet turn out more work. They were amused, then fascinated, as he vigorously demonstrated the efficient way to use a shovel.

He explained his "Law of heavy laboring," which showed that hard muscle work could be done efficiently only if muscles are allowed a certain percentage of time for rest. He had calculated, for instance, that when carrying a ninety pound object, the muscles should be under load only 43 per cent of the time. When this was applied to laborers who were carrying iron, having them take several rests each hour, it was amazing that men who had previously carried twelve and one-half tons each day began to carry forty-seven tons a day, and without harmful effects.

Such testimony made front-page newspaper headlines. Readers, especially business people, found these stories as exciting as the discovery of a new continent. This dramatic investigation and its publicity raised the curtain on a new era of widespread activity in improving efficiency.

II

What necromancy had this man discovered that could bring about almost unbelievable increases in efficiency? Taylor was certainly not a genius. He had no more abilities than many other executives and skilled mechanics of the time.

But Taylor was unusual in his outlook or approach to work. He assumed that the usual way of doing a task was probably inefficient and that it could be improved. Taylor was convinced that an engineering or scientific approach was the only trustworthy means for finding a better way to tackle a task. That is why the name of Scientific Management was given to his work during the congressional hearings.

Taylor's work was wide ranging. He included the entire organization and administration of a business, as well as the pick-and-shovel departments. Accounting, quality control, functional departmentalization, planning, purchasing specifications, inventory control—all were tackled as scientific problems. It seemed revolutionary back in the early 1900's. Today it seems like ordinary common sense.

A large share of the methods used by every business today was developed, to some extent at least, by Taylor at the turn of the century. What we are most interested in now, however, are his findings about methods it is smart for the individual to use for increasing his own efficiency.

III

How did Taylor qualify himself for this new field of professional endeavor? But for a quirk of fortune he would have become a lawyer, as his well-to-do Philadelphia family had planned. He was sent to an expensive school to prepare for college; the intense, conscientious, hard-working youth overworked his eyes, and they failed him shortly after he passed the college entrance examinations. The family physician advised against sending him to college. That closed the door to the law, for which we can be thankful.

So at eighteen he headed in a much different direction, becoming an unpaid apprentice to learn "the art and mystery" of a machine shop. He chose that new direction largely to have something to do—he could not bear being idle—and because it would not require close eye work. After a few months in the machine shop he liked that work so well—ten hours a day, without pay—that although his eyes improved he would not leave. Four years of apprenticeship in the pump factory, and he was qualified as a trained machinist.

Qualified, but no job. A financial depression had brought business almost to a standstill, and the only work he could get was as a day laborer in a Philadelphia steel plant that was famous for making tires for railroad locomotives and for being progressive as mills went in those good old days.

When he reported for work at that progressive mill, after a two and one-half mile walk along the railroad tracks to his job, he entered dilapidated buildings, their windows encrusted with years of soot and grime. The darkness was scarcely penetrated by the smelly kerosene flares that furnished light for the shop—they gave off as much smoke as light. It was cold in winter, sweltering in the humid summer—no place for a softie. A dreary place to work, judging by present-day standards.

And also an inefficient place as young Taylor was quick to observe—especially after the old-timers who systematically "soldiered" at their work told him to slow down, or else. Soon, however, he was boss of these old-timers; a touchy position for any conscientious young man.

Nine years after starting as a laborer he became chief engineer of the mill, which he had already made a much different place to work—the windows were washed regularly, for instance. In the meantime he had, by three hours' study a night, received a degree in mechanical engineering from Stevens Institute of Technology—self-education to increase his own efficiency.

His first achievements were with machines. He improved the efficiency of steam hammers by building a high-speed hammer which did not break down once in the dozen years it was used before being replaced by a larger one. He had developed a steel that would cut metals almost twice as rapidly as other cutting steels.

But as he went on to other companies—paper manufacturing, ball bearings, printing, shipyards, electric motors, farm machinery, concrete products, and more steel mills—he tackled efficiency from other angles. The crying need, he came to feel, was more efficient use of the skills of the individual and better ways for people to work.

IV

An experience at the ball-bearing factory illustrates his early work on the more efficient use of human skills. The girls who inspected the final product worked ten and one-half hours a day peering intently at the bearings under a bright light as they searched for almost invisible defects. It was not physically hard work, but it required close concentration and was very tiring.

Taylor knew from personal experience what it was to have one's eyes fail, and he had observed that the girls idled many times a day to rest their eyes. He became convinced that their workday was too long to be efficient, and decided to shorten it a little at a time and see what happened to their efficiency.

Usually he was blunt and dogmatic, but on this occasion he tried to be tactful with the girls, and failed. They were asked to vote on whether they wished to work only ten hours a day for the same pay they were receiving for ten and one-half hours. All one hundred and twenty girls voted to keep the longer day—they didn't believe the no-pay-cut promise!

Taylor promptly threw tact out the window and shortened their workday anyway. A month later he shortened it another half-hour, and introduced a department-wide rest pause of ten minutes in the forenoon and again in the afternoon.

During this pause the girls could walk around, visit, stretch themselves. Had Taylor enjoyed coffee, the girls might have had a cup. This first coffee break—without coffee—came after the girls had worked about one and one half hours; that was about the time that Sanford E. Thompson, the associate in charge of this experiment, observed that signs of tiring and "nervousness" began to appear.

Now the girls worked less, but efficiency went up. They turned out a third more in nine and one-half hours than they had previously done in ten and one-half hours.

The next month the working day was cut to eight and one-half hours, and the girls were given four coffeeless coffee breaks. They then produced a little more. Obviously, the long working day, with no rest breaks, was self-defeating and inefficient.

Taylor took that experience to heart and began to search for easier —more efficient—ways to use human talents. What he later found seemed unbelievable at the time, and even today many people have difficulty believing they can often be more efficient by working less— until they try it.

V

It seemed "just natural" for Taylor to be efficiency-minded. He certainly was bent on trying to improve almost everything, almost from his cradle. Hell-bent, the neighbors may have thought, as they saw him trying to improve the children's games and toys. They laughed about his boyhood hikes because he would walk for a while with a short stride, then a long stride, trying to find which was better. (We now know that the medium-length stride for each individual's build is the most efficient for that person.)

When he was studying engineering three hours a night—including Sundays—he tried out different hours and methods of study. For a while he got up at 2 A.M. and studied until 5 A.M., after which he took a half-hour nap before leaving for the steel mill. And he had enough self-control to keep that up if it had proven a better way, but he concluded it was more efficient to study in the evening. A quarter-century later psychologists demonstrated that he was right, that more is remembered of what is studied before going to bed than of what is studied shortly after getting up early in the morning.

(Robert G. LeTourneau's experiments to find the best time for him to study should also be noted. He had quit school at the eighth grade, because he was overgrown, six feet tall and felt conspicuous. At twenty-one, when he was chopping oak trees by himself, he felt the need for more schooling and sent for a correspondence course. When

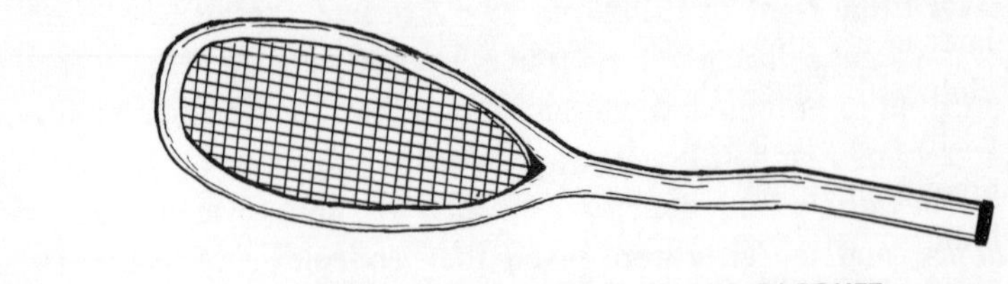

16. TAYLOR'S EFFICIENT TENNIS RACQUET

The offset in the handle enabled him to make an overcut stroke that gave the ball a down-curve so that it bounced in a way to baffle his opponents

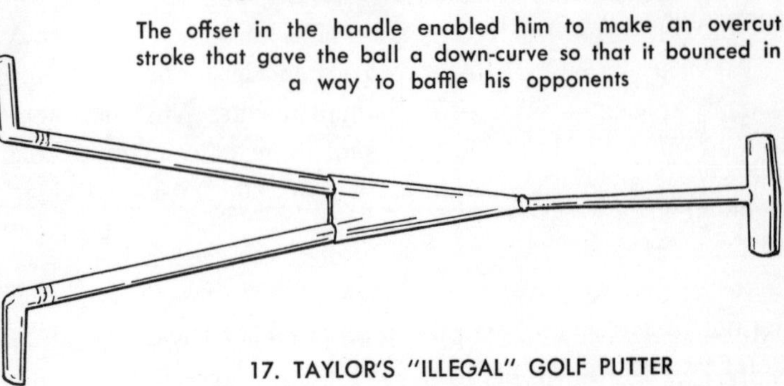

17. TAYLOR'S "ILLEGAL" GOLF PUTTER

This two-handled putter was swung between his feet as he stood squarely behind the ball and facing the hole, to line up the direction accurately.

he tried to study evenings, however, he promptly went to sleep after the twelve hours of chopping. He tried studying early in the morning, but was not wide-awake enough. This is the plan he finally hit upon: From 6 A.M. to 10 A.M. he chopped oak; then he studied four hours, chopping again from 2 P.M. to 6 P.M. That way he got all the chopping done, finished four correspondence courses in one winter, and could go to sleep evenings when he felt like it.)

Taylor's recreations, too, were given the efficiency treatment. Not satisfied with his tennis game, he experimented with racquets and settled on one with a jog in the handle that gave it about a two-inch offset. With this "spoon-handled racquet" he could give the ball a terrific overcut so that its peculiar bounce baffled opponents. When he was twenty-five he won the United States doubles championship, but the Lawn Tennis Association declared his screwball racquet out of bounds for future competitions.

Equally screwball—but efficient—were the golf clubs he devised later in life after he had taken up golf as a recreation. There was one club with which this one hundred and forty-pound sedentary man easily made 250-yard drives. It was his putter, however, that drew the greater attention because of its unusual appearance. It was a two-handled affair, resembling a sawed-off wooden crutch. After some spectacular performances with it, the golf association banned it from competitions.

VI

An interesting characteristic of the men who ushered in our era of efficiency was the attention they devoted to making their homes efficient. Efficiency to them was not something for the job only, but for all living. How delighted they would be with modern homes with all their conveniences! And they would probably go right to work figuring out further improvements on them!

Jefferson filled the mansion he built at Monticello with efficiency ideas. Tourists visit it today not only as a historic shrine but also to observe his efficiency gadgets.

When Taylor built his southern-colonial-style mansion from which he spread the gospel of efficiency there were inevitably many innovations upon which the architects frowned. But Taylor was a man who had his way regardless of architectural traditions—after all, he was sure there was always some better way for everything. Some innovations in his mansion were efficiency-minded, others simply innovations he wanted.

For example, he wanted enormous windows for an unbroken view over the wide valley below, windows starting at the floor, nine feet wide, and pivoted at the sides so they could be tilted to let air circulate yet keep rain out. Picture windows in 1903!

"We can do it, if you insist," the architects protested, "but how will you handle the heavy shutters that will be needed to keep the sun out?" So Taylor designed hydraulic shutters which his wife could operate with an easy touch on a valve—half a century before automobiles had power windows!

His famous boxwood hedge is another example of his ability to dig to the root of a problem and produce a better way as a result. This hedge story is worth a little detail in the telling because it highlights the efficiency value of getting accurate information before acting.

This magnificient hedge was set out exactly a century before by Count John du Barry, and was some nine feet wide and tall as a man could reach. But it was not located where it could be seen from those picture windows. Nursery specialists said the hedge could not be moved; years before they had tried to move some of the hedge bushes, but they invariably died. It's just the nature of boxwood, the specialists said, that it can't be transplanted.

"What about its nature makes it that way?" Taylor asked. They couldn't tell him. He decided to find out for himself what the nature of boxwood was. A trench was dug around one of the shrubs, and a tunnel bored under it. Then, handful by handful, the dirt was pulled away until the first tiny roots were discovered. As they neared the center of the shrub they found why attempts at transplanting had failed.

The three-inch stalk of the shrub did not send down tap roots, as the specialists had presumed all self-respecting shrubs did. Instead, the main roots fanned out like the ribs of an opened umbrella just under the soil. At their ends, three to four feet from the stalk, sprouted pear-shaped tangles of rootlets.

That discovery explained the previous failures. Nurserymen had been digging the conventional ball of dirt, and so had moved only the stem and left the roots behind. After Taylor got to the root of the trouble it was simple to plan how to move the boxwood in great frames which securely held chunks of soil eight feet wide and thirty feet long without disturbing the umbrella of roots.

More directly on the personal efficiency side, he had rudimentary air conditioning in his mansion—and this way back in 1903. Also large concealed elevators that lifted firewood to the three huge fireplaces, the logs pre-positioned and ready to roll on to the fire when a panel in the wall was opened.

VIII

That mansion on Chestnut Hill became the Mecca for efficiency-minded executives, college professors, and high-ranking army and navy officers. Taylor had planned it with that purpose in view. He wanted a headquarters where he could invite men of affairs and mold their thinking efficiency wise. They came in a steady stream; Taylor lectured and explained in his home, then they visited nearby companies that were using his methods.

During the years he had been employed by various firms his work had to be done in comparative secrecy. The firms quite naturally did not want their competitors to catch on. A trade secret, they always say, is worth more than a patent. Competitors realized that wonders were being accomplished, but were pretty much in the dark about how they were being done.

That is one reason why Taylor decided in 1901 that "I can no longer work for money." He let a couple of years pass after he quit and during these stand-by years changes in ownership and processes made his findings no longer the precious trade secrets they had been, so he could feel free to tell about their "art and mystery" to whomever he could interest. He wanted to improve the efficiency of all business by educating business leaders and developing specialists for the work.

It was easier for Taylor to talk face to face than to write. It took him months to write a report that a country newspaper editor would peck out in a couple of hours. It was not until 1911 that his book, *The Principles of Scientific Management*, was published. What an impact it made after that congressional investigation—within two years it was translated into nine languages.

At last the Era of Efficiency was under way in offices and factories. Individuals, however, were slower to organize their lives so they could make fuller use of their capacities. Even today many individuals lag in using efficient methods that could help them achieve more for themselves.

5. The Gilbreths' Motion Economy for Efficiency

I

"SHE GOES THROUGH THE MOTIONS OF WORKING, BUT DOESN'T GET much done," neighborhood wives often say as they chuckle about a bride's housekeeping. Her flutter of activity keeps her much busier than she should be because she goes through many motions that do not help toward keeping her love nest shipshape and meals ready on schedule. But give her a few months and she will probably do the work with fewer motions and better results, just as the amused neighbors learned how not to make too many detours while doing their daily chores.

And their amusement might change to embarrassment if a motion-economy expert studied their own ways of doing housework. Many studies have revealed that experienced housewives are likely to go through twice as many motions as are needed for most of their tasks.

Consider preparing meals, which was one household detail studied by Wayne State University in Michigan homes. The average housewife took 500 steps, stooped down twelve times, and reached up fifty times while preparing a meal. But by planning the work and rearranging the equipment, three-fourths of the stepping, stooping, and stretching were eliminated—motion economy.

There is more to motion economy, however, than reducing the

number of motions. As every golfer quickly finds out, some motions are more effective than others.

Mopping a floor, for example, can be improved most by using motions that are more effective than the usual push-and-pull. The way experts recommend is to (a) stand with feet far apart, (b) swing the mop from side to side in an arc, (c) no stopping at the end of the stroke, instead keep on moving the mop in a looping turn (hairpin curve) into position for the next strip of floor. Keep on swinging it from side to side, (d) steadily walking backward slowly, and (e) from time to time flip the mop over when looping at the end of an arc so that a fresh surface is in contact with the floor.

As a general *guide,* gently curving motions are more efficient than zigzag or straight back-and-forth motions, because of the way our bones, joints, and muscles are put together.

II

Motion economy does not require more rapid movements; the harassed bride is probably doing just that, and the result is commotion rather than effective motion. Only a few slowpokes need to speed up. What most of us need, for most of the things we do, is (a) plan our work so it can be done with the fewest motions, and then (b) do it with the kind of motions that are easiest and bring the best results.

Driving nails illustrates the importance of finesse in using motions that bring results easiest. The professional carpenter has picked up the know-how of making hammering motions that get results easiest; he seldom works as rapidly as the amateur tries to, but he gets better results. Let's watch an amateur and a carpenter drive nails.

The amateur holds the hammer near the middle of its handle, the professional holds it by the very end. By holding it at the end, the professional magnifies the muscular force he puts into the start of each blow—nails are driven in more rapidly. This also helps him guide the hammer more accurately—no nails bent or missed.

The amateur nail driver bears down with his arm muscles all the way. His arm remains so stiff that when the hammer lands on the nail a shock from the impact is telegraphed to his shoulder joint—result, sore shoulder tomorrow, in addition to needless muscle tiredness. But the professional bears down only at the beginning of the blow. He gives the hammer a vigorous start, then lets its momentum do the work while he mostly guides the hammer the last half of the swing. By the time the hammer strikes his arm is fairly relaxed and the impact does not jar his shoulder joint.

After that impact the professional lets the hammer bounce upward of its own accord; he scarcely has to lift it because the recoil does much of the lifting for him. But the amateur usually comes to a dead stop after each impact. With the amateur it is bang-stop-lift, then bang-stop-lift all over again. But with the professional it is swing-relax-bounce, swing-relax-bounce.

Rhythm, which is important in repetitive operations, is put into the professional's hammering. The amateur seldom has rhythm because of the dead stop he makes after hitting—or perhaps missing!—the nail. The professional strikes in rhythmic cycles, in march time, with the accent on the part of the cycle where the hammer is upraised and he begins the blow forcefully. With mopping, the side-to-side rhythm is produced by looping instead of coming to a stop, and by putting the emphasis or accent on starting the return swing just after looping.

A guide: In most work where movements are repeated it is more efficient to avoid dead stops and repeat the moves in a steady rhythm with the accent at the point where most strength should be applied. The place to grunt is at the accent.

III

Those are some of the hundreds of practical examples of motion economy, which was originated by a russet-haired human dynamo, Frank B. Gilbreth. He was consumed by a desire to get things done in better ways. From the age of seventeen he devoted his life to this, first as a practical builder and later in laboratory studies. His unusual life and accomplishments are of particular significance to the person who wants to increase his own personal efficiency.

So wrapped up was Gilbreth in getting things done that in his late twenties, and making money hand over fist, he resolved never to get married. Marriage would interfere with his important work, said this man who charmed the ladies without trying.

This heavyweight from Down East showed signs of weakening when a slender California girl with titian-tinted tresses came to visit relatives in Boston. Willowy Lillian Moller wanted to see the historic spots around Boston; Frank hurried her around to look at construction jobs instead. She liked to read and write verse; he talked mostly bricks and cement. She listened, and he began to feel certain that he had at last discovered a woman who was interested in such practical topics, and it added to her winsome fascination. Good-by, resolve!

Lillian and Frank Gilbreth made an amazing team, in professional work and in their home life. Lillian did become deeply interested in his work on efficiency. This man who worked like a fiend had found a way to lay bricks with only four and one-half motions instead of eighteen—350 bricks an hour instead of the 120 by old-fashioned wasteful methods. She thought that was almost as good as being able to write a poem.

She became so intrigued by the significance of such accomplishments that she decided to get a doctor's degree in psychology to prepare herself to work with him in the quest for better work methods. Frank had the engineer's and practical construction man's approach to efficiency, now his wife could add the psychological approach—a combination of approaches it is difficult to beat, especially when used by such a capable team.

IV

Motion economy was started by Frank Gilbreth as an obvious, common-sense thing to do. He had come from a small town on the Kennebec River in Maine, where his father ran the hardware store and was the big man in the small community. His parents and most of the villagers were of Puritan and Pilgrim stock.

In such a place Yankee ingenuity, hatred of idleness, and disgust at waste were in the air. The boy breathed deeply, and caught a severe and permanent case of all three.

His mother moved near Boston after his father's death, for better educational facilities for the children—the Yankee gift for helping children make the most of their capacities. The estate seemed adequate, but investments turned out poorly, as they sometimes do for widows. When Frank attended high school his resourceful mother was taking in boarders to help support the family.

Although he had passed the entrance examinations to Massachusetts Institute of Technology, at seventeen and fresh from high-school graduation, he bought a pair of mason's overalls, got a union card, and went to work to learn bricklaying. College would have strained the family's dwindling resources, so he thriftily decided to learn engineering the practical way on construction jobs supplemented by night-school courses. When Gilbreth began his apprenticeship in Boston, Frederick W. Taylor was already shop manager of the steelworks in Philadelphia and trying out some of his ideas of scientific management.

Gilbreth's first hot day as a bricklayer's apprentice was confusing. Four bricklayers showed him how—and each showed him a different way. He also noticed that each instructor showed him a different way than he used himself. And to compound the confusion, during the day each bricklayer changed his own methods from time to time. Which was the right way?

That night his bones ached, and the next morning his muscles were sore. There must be some way to cut down all that stooping and stretching, he thought. And there must be some motions that are better than others for laying bricks. His Yankee ingenuity went to work on such practical questions.

He designed a new kind of scaffold that first year, one that was easily raised or lowered so that much of the stooping and lifting were eliminated—more bricks laid with fewer and easier motions. He began to show an eagle eye for spotting waste motions and an ability to form mental images of better motions. To improve his own motion skills he trained himself to use either hand for almost any task.

At twenty-two he was made job superintendent, and began to look forward to joining the partnership. Three years later he realized it was a closed corporation and that he had no chance of becoming a partner. He cut loose and set up his own contracting business, starting small as a specialist in basement construction and waterproofing.

But he had big hopes and a Down East inclination not to let bankers get control of his growing business. His invention of a gravity concrete mixer provided the funds to widen his contracting. The mixer was sold by the thousand—it was used in building the New York City subways—and he had factories making it in six countries.

Soon he was leading a whirlwind existence, as one of the largest independent builders in the United States. When a durable building was needed in a hurry, corporations turned to this man who had trained an organization which operated by a secret manual he had written. A skyscraper in Seattle, a powerhouse in Michigan, a women's club in Boston, an entire town in Maine, for instance. He would have big building projects under way in all four corners of the country at once. He kept tabs on the work by travel and by daily photographs mailed from the jobs for him to study.

Speed construction, it came to be called. It was speedy beyond doubt, but the name was unfortunate. Speed suggests flimsy jerry-building, but he built for durability and quality. Speed construction also suggests driving the workers, but Gilbreth's speed was obtained by the opposite method—by using fewer but more effective motions and other efficiency methods which were carefully guarded in the secret manual. New methods were often hit upon as he studied the photographs mailed in from the field.

His wish to do quality building kept him from bidding for jobs. Builders are said to be tempted to neglect quality in order to make a profit on a bid they figured too closely. But Gilbreth used actual cost plus a fixed fee, an unusual method in those day, and not common now. Not cost plus a percentage, which might tempt a contractor to let costs go up, but cost plus a definite fee. He charged a stiff fee, but firms who were in a hurry paid it, knowing they would get an honestly-made building, and more quickly than any other way.

The wide-ranging construction jobs demanded lots of travel, as much as seventy thousand miles a year, and this before airlines. Although he worked during much of his travel time—he had a driver for his automobile so he could work on auto trips—the incessant travel interfered with getting some of the things done he wanted to do. More than that, the longer trips were keeping him from his family—this dynamo who a few years before was not going to marry.

V

As he turned forty, two motives became irresistible: to make motion economy a laboratory science so it could be based upon more than shrewd common sense and ingenuity; to be with his family more and help bring up the children efficiently. The contracting tapered off and he eagerly shifted his limitless energies into the world's first full-time laboratory and consulting work on motion economy. This was when Lillian started to study for her doctor's degree in order to work with him; she wrote her thesis with five children in the house. This change in career, it might be called, was made just about the time the Congressional Committee was beginning to learn from Taylor about the great strides that were being made in improving factory efficiency.

Lillian and Frank Gilbreth proceeded to make motion stand still so it could be analyzed. The photographs he had had made of his construction jobs may have given them the starting idea. For the laboratory study they made photographs of work movements, attaching a flash-light bulb to a worker's hand and making a time exposure during a cycle of the work from start to finish, such as one full blow and bounce back to starting position when hammering. The streak of light on the time exposure revealed the path the operator's hands followed, and was called a *cyclegraph.*

Life-size wire models were made of these streaks of light and used to show workers the motions that produced the best results. Examples of these are shown in the illustration for the simple task of using a drill press to make a hole in a piece of metal.

When they wanted to find out about the time as well as the form of the motion, the light bulb on the worker's hand was made to flash ten times a second—about ten times as many flashes as the turn signals on your automobile. Each flash produced a pear-shaped blob on the cyclegraph, showing just how far the hand had moved in one-tenth second. From such a *chronocyclegraph* it was found that it took longer to make a sudden change of direction (push-pull type) than to make a looping turn of direction.

They devised special motion-picture cameras for making *micro-motion analysis,* with the time shown in 1/300 of a second. Movies of a worker were taken with the camera running at high speed, then the motions he had used were studied one picture at a time, revealing moves that were too quick or dexterous for the naked eye to see. This was the granddaddy of the slow-motion pictures which are now sometimes used to entertain movie audiences.

Blueprints of the entire sequence of separate operations needed in doing a particular job were also devised. These *process charts* were

18. A CYCLEGRAPH

The white tangle of lines shows her hand motions in putting on one overshoe. A small light bulb was attached to each wrist. The cyclegraph begins at the lower right where she picked the overshoe from the floor. (Courtesy Eagle-Picher Company)

19. CYCLEGRAPH MODELS

Wire models of cyclegraphs of arm movement in working at a drill press. Model at the left shows motions used by an unskilled worker. The others show how he used fewer and fewer movements as he gained in efficiency at this work.

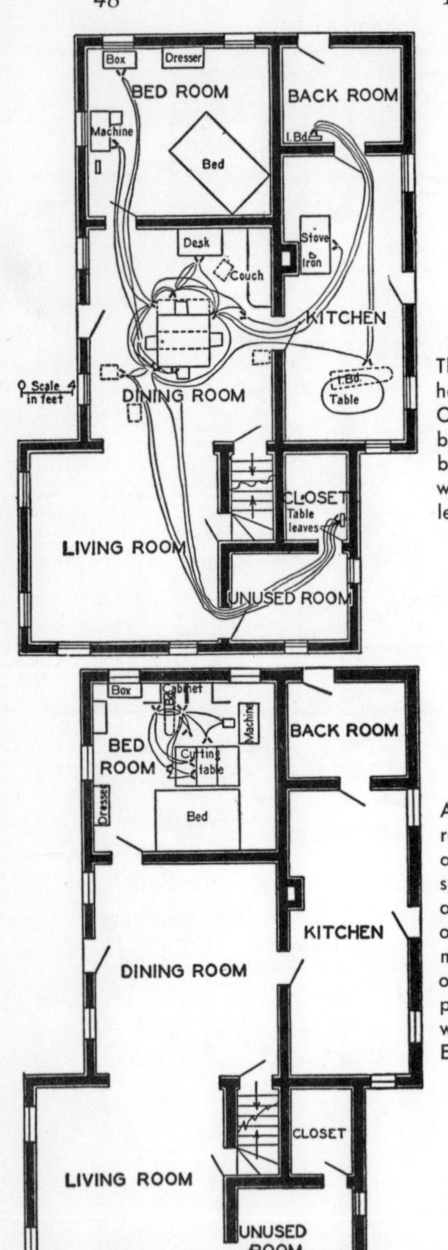

20. THE ORIGINAL SEWING PLAN

The housewife may save money by sewing at home but usually she does not save herself. On the left, we see traced the steps taken by one woman in making an apron in assembling the material, doing the really productive work, and later putting away the extra table leaves, iron, and such.

21. THE NEW ARRANGEMENT

A homemade cabinet about the size of a wardrobe cabinet was put in the bedroom to house all the items used in sewing, even including a special lightweight folding table for cutting and basting; this is shown on the right. The original plan required walking 524 feet to make the apron. The rearranged plan required only 40 feet of walking. Similar thoughtful planning will make great savings in most housework. (Courtesy Cornell University Agricultural Experiment Station; work of Ella Cushman) useful for highlighting steps that could be combined or eliminated. Such as holding off making a telephone call the instant one thinks of it, and waiting until several calls can be made in one batch.

Road maps, or *flow diagrams,* were also devised to accomplish much the same purpose as process charts for the person who has difficulty visualizing. A flow diagram pictures the sequence of operations, or steps taken, by lines on a drawing of the floor space.

When a flow diagram was made at Cornell University of the job of making an apron at home, it was found that the farm woman walked 524 feet in getting materials and such. Using that flow diagram to locate the wasteful parts of the arrangement, a plan was worked out that made it possible to make the apron by walking only 40 feet.

A Vermont farmer made a flow diagram of the sequence of operations he followed while doing his daily chores around the barnyard and hen house. By working out simpler methods in pencil on the flow chart the five hours and forty four minutes he had been spending on these chores each day was cut down to two hours and five minutes. Originally he had walked three and one-quarter miles a day in doing the chores; under the new method it was only one and one quarter miles—motion economy!

The flow diagram is one of the best friends an efficiency-minded person can have, especially if he cannot visualize as vividly as Gilbreth could. Use a flow diagram to help find a better way for any task, or to make a home or work place more convenient. Follow these steps: (a) Start by drawing a floor plan to scale; (b) then locate the equipment on it, also to scale; (c) now draw pencil lines to make a road map of the steps you would have to take with that arrangement; (d) then study out a different arrangement and make a road map of the steps needed; (e) finally decide on the method the flow diagrams indicate will use the least motions and the easiest motions.

VI

When Gilbreth visited an industrial exposition in London he paused at an exhibit in which the manufacturer had one of his speediest workers pasting labels on boxes of his product. She was attractive to watch, of course, and the many onlookers were also impressed by her speed. But not Gilbreth.

After watching her work a few moments, irrepressible Gilbreth stepped forward and said to the girl, "You are not doing that the best way."

Ignoring her astonishment and murmurs from the crowd, he showed her a different way that almost doubled her output. He could do wonders without a flow diagram or cyclegraph to visualize for him.

That incident illustrates what is probably the most important equipment the average person needs to practice motion economy. Simply *be motion-economy-minded*—regarding your own work as well as the work of others; too often we can see that the other person is making useless motions but neglect to watch ourselves. You do not need a laboratory, or a vast amount of technical information, but you do need to have this aspect of efficiency-mindedness.

Gilbreth was undoubtedly one of the most motion-economy-minded persons who ever lived. He was always looking for ways to save motion, and usually able to find a way or two after watching a job for a few minutes, as in the London incident.

He was motion-economy-minded in his personal and home life, too. He used a shaving brush in each hand to lather his broad face; he also tried shaving with an old-fashioned straight-edged razor in each hand but that was not a success. (This was before the days of safety or electric razors, which he would have acclaimed—and perhaps improved.)

He tested various methods of buttoning his vest, and found it more efficient to start buttoning at the bottom and work upward. (General U. S. Grant solved this problem by not buttoning his vests; even as president at formal dinners he appeared in unbuttoned vests, and his wife had to draw him to one side and button them.)

Gilbreth figured how to bathe with the fewest motions, and taught the method to his children as soon as they were old enough to bathe themselves and the total saving could be considerable with his large number of children to use the bath.

A process chart on the bathroom wall also showed the children the best sequence of operations for brushing their teeth.

Idle time was to be used, too, just as he worked while traveling. A chart of the Morse code hung in the bathroom, and soon the children were tapping messages in code to themselves and to their parents. A phonograph with French and German records was in the bathroom.

He took movies of the children washing dishes, and together they planned better ways which not only made the chore easier but also less like drudgery to the youngsters.

He devised an improved flow diagram for surgical operations, and it is still followed in its essentials in most hospitals. When his own tonsils were removed he watched the operation in a mirror, and had motion pictures taken to study later. But the cameraman was "operation shy" and forgot to remove the dust cap from the lens.

"There is no waste in the world," he said, "that equals the waste from needless, ill-directed, and ineffective motions."

Fortunately, the waste can easily be corrected, once the individual becomes motion-economy-minded. Probably there is not a person in the world who could not make great improvements in this direction. A smart place to begin is with the tasks that take the most of your time, or the tasks that you dislike the most.

6. How to Light for Easier Seeing

I

ENVIRONMENTAL CONDITIONS HAVE POWERFUL INFLUENCES ON OUR efficiency. The conditions do not have to be extreme to help or lower our efficiency. For instance, if you read for three hours during an evening with the light coming directly down from a ceiling fixture you will have nine times as much loss in ability to maintain clear vision as if you read in diffused indirect light of the same brightness.

Anything in the environment that makes a person uncomfortable is likely to lower his personal efficiency. It may lower efficiency because physiological processes are handicapped, or because the discomfort distracts us so we "can't keep the mind on the work." Dr. Guy P. Crowden emphasized the physiological processes when he told the Royal Institute of Public Health and Hygiene, "Sensations of discomfort are really warnings that some factors are adversely affecting the body and need adjustment and control."

Environmental conditions which are known to influence comfort, well-being, and working efficiency are:

Lighting
Temperature
Noise
Seating
Clothing, including shoes

Most homes, offices, and factories do not provide the efficiency-promoting environments they could. That is especially true of lighting, which is below what it should be in practically all homes and in about half the factories and offices.

Lighting is below what it should be when these things happen: You have to turn your back to the light to read comfortably. The light makes you squint. You have to move to a brighter location to read a number in the telephone directory. Your eyes "get tired" after a couple of hours of reading. You can work faster and with less effort in daylight than under the artificial light.

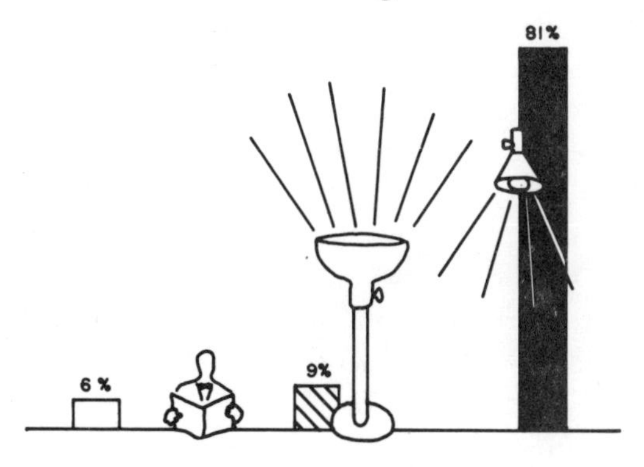

In daylight (least blurring) — In diffused lighting — Under direct lighting (most blurring)

(Data from Drs. Clarence E. Ferree and Gertrude Rand)

22. LOSS OF CAPACITY TO SEE CLEARLY AFTER READING THREE HOURS

Of all the environmental conditions that influence our efficiency, lighting is the one that is easiest to have right. Lighting helps personal efficiency when it can pass these five requirements which have been established by numerous researches:

1. The over-all appearance should be attractive.
2. The light should be fairly uniform throughout the room.
3. It should be as bright as outside daylight on a slightly cloudy day.
4. The light should be diffused and not cause noticeable shadows.
5. The light sources should not be naked.

II

When the housekeeper uses ornamental shades to "decorate with light," she is aiming in the right direction—but she should be careful to decorate so the other four requirements can be passed.

An environment that is attractive is conducive to personal efficiency. There may be a few eccentric people who can work well in a dusty attic or cluttered room, but most people do better when their surroundings please the eye—please it in every way, as listed above.

Dr. Warner Brown, at the University of California, made one of the first tests that demonstrated the usefulness of working in attractive surroundings. He had one group of people work in a dingy, attic-like room and another group did similar work in an attractive room. Those in the unattractive room did not accomplish as much.

Some of the wide-ranging effects of attractive surroundings were brought out in more recent experiments by Drs. Norbett L. Mintz and Abraham H. Maslow, at Brandeis University. There was more monotony, more tiredness, more headaches, more sleepiness, more discontent, more irritability, and more hostile feelings in the ugly room.

An attractive workplace obviously does more than merely please the eye. It might be said to bring out the best in the person.

Artificial light can be used in more ways than decorative lamps and shades to add to the attractiveness. For example, preference should be given to lights that give off a yellowish or "warm" tint, as most incandescent bulbs do. Bluish or greenish tints produce a "cold" and unattractive appearance; some of them distort the color of make-up so that beautiful girls look ghoulish.

This is particularly true of the light from fluorescent tubes, which give more light from less electricity, are popular in business places, and come in a variety of colors. Restaurant owners have discovered that food looks unappetizing when bluish tubes are used; special tube colors have been developed to make food look appealing.

We will come back to some other ways lighting affects attractiveness as we describe how to meet some of the other requirements.

III

Light should be of fairly uniform intensity throughout the room, whether home, office, or factory. Whenever eyes are being used in work or reading, *the entire visual field should be evenly lighted*—no bright spots or dark corners. Nature lights the outdoors uniformly, and we should try to duplicate that indoors. If one corner of the room is kept dark in order to see television, for instance, the light is not suited to reading.

Here are some ways to take advantage of natural light to have more uniform daytime lighting inside a room. It is fairly easy in a very small room. But if the room is large enough that someone has to work ten feet from a window, that person will probably need some artificial light, even on a bright day.

It helps very much to get the light into the far parts of a room if the ceiling is white and the walls are as light colored as possible.

The daylight that comes through the upper half of the window goes farthest to brighten up the back corners. Most people like to have the window shades pulled partway down for appearance, but the light will be more efficient if the shades are rolled up to the top during seeing hours. Awnings, which are sometimes necessary, cut down the light from the top half of the windows; this can be offset, but only slightly, if the underside of the awning is white and the ends are open. And keep the awnings raised except when the sun strikes the windows.

When you plan a new home, look into the possibility of putting the windows closer to the ceiling than is conventional. The nearer they are to the ceiling, the brighter and more uniform the natural daylight that floods the room.

Also, the more windows in a room the brighter and more evenly is natural light distributed. When there are windows in more than one side of the room it is still better, for ventilation as well as for natural lighting.

When using artificial light it is essential to have the light sources scattered through the room to make the lighting more even. *Always use several small lights in preference to one large one.* This also helps you decorate with light.

As an example, in our living room we have no ceiling lights. We depend upon six movable small lamps, three fixed lights on pictures, and in addition fluorescent ("warm"-colored) tubes that are concealed in open-top valences on the four regular windows and the ten-foot picture windows.

Students commonly study with only a reading lamp which is directed on the table top, leaving the remainder of the room in semidarkness. Some do this intentionally, believing it helps them concentrate if they are unable to see anything except the study-table top.

This is a mistake in every way. Other lights should be turned on in the study room; enough other lights so that with a 75-watt bulb in the reading lamp you can read fine print without having to strain.

In offices and factories continuous strips of fluorescent tubes are commonly used to make the lighting fairly uniform. Workers tend to complain, however, that the lighting is monotonous or unnatural, especially if bluish tubes are used. These complaints are also partly owing to the fact that there are only bare walls and machines to look at—not attractive surroundings.

Some companies solve this problem by painting the machines in pleasing colors to give what interior decorators call "visual interest" to the room. After all, although the outdoors is uniformly lighted, there are areas of colors to give the visual interest which makes the outdoors more attractive.

IV

The light should be bright enough at the point of work so you can see what you have to without effort or strain—almost *as bright as outdoors on a day that is slightly cloudy.* Very few homes can meet this requirement except when the direct sunlight happens to stream into a room. Most of the newer school buildings and new offices and factories pass this test.

The brightness of light needed depends partly upon what the eyes are being used for. For leisurely conversation the brightness seldom matters—easier to fall in love, it has been said, in dim light. But if you have to thread a needle, better have about thirty foot-candles of light on the needle. For studying and similar reading, the recommended brightness is fifteen foot-candles. After about age fifty, most people need brighter light for easy reading.

How bright is a foot-candle? You can get some idea from this: an ordinary bridge lamp with a paper shade and a 50-watt bulb produces three foot-candles fifty inches from the bulb. Far from adequate for easy seeing, yet that is what many people hope to read by. (Direct sunshine is 8,000 foot-candles, and will "burn your eyes.")

The larger electric-utility companies have lighting engineers who can easily measure the foot-candles you are getting at present, and they can make suggestions for bringing your lighting up to standard.

You can get a picture of what is needed for ordinary—not close—eye work from the way my workroom is lighted. The room is 15 feet by 18 feet, with four large windows which fill two-thirds of the outside wall. The white window shades are left at the top until the sun strikes a window. The ceiling is white, the walls a very light green, which reflects about 70 per cent of the light that falls on them. That is the natural lighting.

The artificial lighting comes from ten "warm-" colored fluorescent tubes of 40 watts each; unless it is a bright day outside, I work with four of the tubes lighted during the day. In addition, a movable 200-watt semi-indirect floor lamp is at the settle, and a movable 60-watt incandescent lamp is at the desk for reading fine print. Despite all those lights, the room is lighted barely up to standard.

Surveys have shown that the home rooms which are most dangerously underlighted are the kitchen and the bathroom. The former may partly account for the 40 per cent of home accidents which occur in the kitchen.

When you travel you will be wise to take along a couple 100-watt bulbs in your baggage. Many hotel and motel rooms are inadequately lighted, and if you have to write reports, or want to get your make-up on straight, use your own bulbs.

There are several ways to increase the daylight brightness of a room without using more lights. In the average suburb, for instance, a window that goes unwashed for six months admits only half as much light—wash up the windows to brighten up inside. Many factories have full-time window-washing crews to improve the natural lighting and also to make the place more attractive. Other factories that are located in smoky districts have given up trying to keep ahead of the grime and simply use more artificial light.

Draperies that hang partly over the glass cut down the light greatly; sometimes more than never-washed windows. This can be changed by using longer rods, or drapery cranes, which allow the drapes to be drawn back far enough to clear the glass; this also makes the room look larger as well as brighter.

Window curtains, even sheer ones, reduce the entering daylight considerably. Dark-colored window shades block off daylight as if there were no windows behind them. When you get new shades, select white and semi-transparent ones, and leave them as high up the window as your aesthetic taste allows. For sleeping rooms, however, use white but opaque shades so that the rooms can be darkened for daytime naps.

Window air conditioners and window fans play havoc with the natural light in a room. There is no way to solve this except to increase the artificial lighting during the daytime hours the room is used for eye work. If fluorescent tubes are used, they will not heat up the room so much as incandescent bulbs.

Do you live in a separate house? Then look around and see if a foundation shrub has grown to cover part of a window. Sometimes the lower limb of a tree blocks off a window so that little light can come in.

Do you use a basement room? It will get considerably more natural daylight if the inside of the window well is painted white.

Do you live in an apartment with windows opening on an inside court? These windows would let in much more light if the landlord painted the court walls white. Next best way to get more daylight through those windows is to fasten a piece of white waterproof hardboard on the outside of the window sill; the board should be as wide as the window, sticking out about two feet, and tilted slightly upward at the far edge so it reflects daylight into the window.

The amount of light, whether natural daylight or artificial, also depends greatly upon the wall colors. As the following table shows, if your walls are dark red you should use about twice as many artificial lights as if the walls were light green.

You will have better light if you select a color from the top of that list—and then mix about an equal amount of white in with it.

Glossy finishes, surprisingly, do not make a room so light as the same color in a flat finish. This is because some of the light is trapped in the finish itself to produce the glossy appearance.

The light reflected into the room from the walls diminishes month by month—dirt steadily accumulates on the walls. Give preference to wall finishes that can be washed, and wash them before they look as if they needed it. Rough plaster is a worse dirt collector than smooth plaster.

A white ceiling is always desirable, to reflect the most possible light downward to reading or work surfaces.

How wall colors affect room lighting:

	Per cent of light it reflects into room
White—new	82 to 89
White—old	75 to 85
Cream	62 to 80
Ivory	73 to 78
Yellow	61 to 75
Light green	48 to 75
Buff	49 to 66
Pink	36 to 61
Light blue	34 to 61
Dark tan	30 to 46
Grays	17 to 63
Dark red	13 to 30
Dark green	11 to 25
Brown wood stain	17 to 29

Incandescent bulbs and fluorescent tubes are usually installed and forgotten until they burn out. The fact is that they give a little less light each week if they are neglected. A month's dust, for instance, reduces their lighting power by around 10 per cent on the average.

All bulbs and tubes should be cleaned about every two weeks, depending upon the dust and grease in the air; kitchen bulbs need cleaning every week in case much frying is done. A clean, damp cloth is usually sufficient, but in the kitchen soap and water may be needed. Take the bulbs and tubes out of the sockets to clean them, and be sure the metal parts are thoroughly dry before putting them back. They can be dusted right in their sockets, but dusting is not always adequate.

The bulbs and tubes themselves deteriorate steadily, giving out less and less light because of the blackish deposit that collects inside the glass. When cleaning them look for black clouds in the ends, and discard those in which it can be easily seen.

Shades, and especially the reflectors used with indirect lights, also need regular cleaning to maintain the lighting at the level it used to be.

Fluorescent tubes and reflectors, or diffusers, do not need cleaning as often as incandescent ones. This is because the fluorescent does not generate so much heat to produce air currents which suck dust to the tube.

V

Hold a pencil about six inches above this page, and parallel to the page. Can you see the pencil shadow plainly? Too bad if you do, because the light in which you use your eyes *should not produce noticeable shadows.*

Direct light, such as is produced by a bridge lamp, most study lamps, or direct sunlight, invariably causes easily noticed shadows. Direct light is harsh.

Diffused light, such as comes from indirect-light fixtures, properly shaded fluorescent tubes, or daylight, is relatively shadowless. Diffused light is soft.

Diffused light is more efficient to work under. Here is the loss of ability to maintain clear vision after three hours use of the eyes under various degrees of diffusion:

Daylight; most diffused	6 per cent loss
Diffused indirect electric light	9 " " "
Less diffused, semi-indirect electric light ...	72 " " "
Direct electric light	81 " " "

The most certain way to have diffused light is to use completely indirect lighting—fixtures that reflect all the direct rays from the bulbs or tubes to the ceiling and upper walls. This requires two or more times as much wattage as when the light rays are directed downward. The reflectors of totally indirect lights are excellent dust catchers and require frequent washing. But totally indirect lighting comes closest to matching the easy seeing of daylight.

The next best way, and usually acceptable in homes, is to use semi-indirect light sources—part of the light is reflected to the ceiling and part down into the room. The fluorescent tubes concealed in open-top window valences at all the windows in our house, for example, throw part of their light to the ceiling, part of it down toward the floor. (Our bedside lamps are totally indirect: a fluorescent tube runs the entire width of the headboard and is fastened to the rear of the headboard, throwing its light up the wall behind the bed. This requires a light wall color to reflect—diffuse—as much as possible of the light from the tube.)

Clear glass bulbs should never be used in homes, or anywhere except under special circumstances. The inside frosted incandescent bulbs give a slightly diffused light right at the source, though not nearly so diffused as even a semi-indirect light fixture.

When direct lighting has to be used, it helps to use several small ones in preference to a single large one. Instead of a 200-watt bulb dangling in the middle of the room, for instance, use 60-watt bulbs in four bridge or table lamps scattered around the room. All inside frost bulbs, of course.

The student who uses an ordinary desk lamp with a 100-watt bulb would be better off to use a lamp at each end of his study table with a 60-watt bulb in each—inside frosted, of course. His eyes would work best, as the preceding table shows, if he studied under totally indirect light.

VI

Can you see well after the headlights of an oncoming automobile hit you in the eyes? Do spots dance in your eyes after you accidentally look at the sun? Have you had a headache after working a short time near an unshaded electric bulb that struck your eyes? Those every day experiences illustrate why *light sources should be invisible.*

The direct rays of light from the white-hot filament of the common incandescent bulb can, almost literally, burn the sensitive retina at the back of the eye. The fluorescent tubes are not so harmful in this respect, since their rays are spread over a larger area at the tube and are not concentrated at one intense point.

Every incandescent bulb should have its burning filament hidden from view. This can usually be accomplished by using shades which still allow much of the light to filter through yet keep the filament safely under cover. Lamps should also be placed where the filament is not likely to be in anyone's line of sight—sit beside it, or in front of it, not behind it. The filament may be hidden when you sit down but hit you in the eye if you are standing up—then either the height of the lamp should be changed, or a round diffuser of, say, fiber glass, used to cover the part that strikes the eye when you stand up.

Every fluorescent tube in a home should have the light from its glowing tube diffused by a honeycomb or grille of some sort. In business and public buildings which have high ceilings this is not so necessary, but in homes it is a must.

Attention should also be given to glittering or shiny objects that are in the direct rays of either the sun or artificial-light source. These can reflect the rays back into the eye, producing glare. A college student was puzzled about the headaches he got after studying about an hour. He had his eyes tested, but did not need glasses. On his study table he had a picture of his mother, and the polished silver frame bounced the light from the filament directly into his eyes. Moving the picture a few inches to one side cured his headaches.

People who have to drive automobiles are often distracted by the glare as the chromium on the steering wheel reflects the sun's rays into their eyes. Some people who drive a great deal have the chromium parts covered with a flat paint that harmonizes with the interior finish and removes the cause of glare.

Housewives have to work with innumerable shiny objects that can produce glare unless the light is well diffused. The kitchen alone is full of them: silverware, dishes, pots and pans, porcelain, polished knobs, and appliances. There will be no appreciable glare from these, however, if all filaments are hidden and all tubes are behind diffusers.

It's smart to make your lighting attractive, fairly uniform throughout the room, as bright as a slightly cloudy day outdoors, diffused and shadowless, with no naked bulbs or tubes to strike you in the eye.

7. How to Use Your Eyes Efficiently

I

WE USE OUR EYES EVERY WAKING MINUTE, ALTHOUGH CLEAR AND easy seeing is not always needed. Many eat breakfast with their eyes only half-open. We can talk over the telephone, walk around in familiar places, daydream or plan, and do many little routine chores even though our vision is blurred.

Most occupations, however, require clear seeing most of the time. Dr. Morris S. Viteles, industrial psychologist at the University of Pennsylvania, has reported surveys that showed the average factory or office job required serious eye work nearly three-fourths of the workday.

Efficiency in seeing has become a problem over the years because human eyes are built so that they see easiest when objects are at some distance away, and fairly sizable. But today most occupations require just the opposite—fairly continuous looking at objects only a foot or two away, and small details have to be noticed quickly, such as the difference between three and eight in the telephone directory. Continuous reading, sewing, typing, bookkeeping, assembly work, could be said to require unnatural seeing.

Very close eye work—where objects are a foot or less from the eye—is required by a few occupations in which small details are important. Examples are watch or radio repairing, dentist and surgeon, and many inspectors and machine adjusters.

Only a few occupations do not demand a great deal of close eye work—farmers, houseworkers, laborers, automobile, and truck drivers. Even these require close eye work at times, as when a laborer uses a level or foot rule.

The six muscles that move each eye function most naturally when we are looking straight ahead. When we close the eyes to relax, or go to sleep they automatically turn upward. Telephone switchboard operators and automobile drivers can look mostly straight ahead, which is the easy direction to look. Most occupations, however, require downward looking for hour after hour.

Although close work and looking downward are harder work for eyes, they can usually take it if the lighting is favorable and the eyes are used properly. Drs. Leonard Carmichael and Walter F. Dearborn found that high-school and college students could read steadily (close eye work, looking downward) for as much as six hours at a stretch without serious ill effects. Those who had to wear glasses did as well as the others.

Whether one needs glasses or not, there are several habits everyone should form which will greatly improve their efficiency in seeing. We will describe those that are of particular usefulness for seeing at less than arm's length, and these include most workaday seeing.

II

You have probably tried to read a newspaper when it was spread out flat on the table in front of you, so you know how difficult it is. It was bothersome partly because you had to look downward, but there is something else of importance. You could read the headline in big type at the top of the page easily enough, but had to lean forward and use effort to read the opening paragraphs at the top of the columns.

You had to lean forward because the eye has an *efficient focusing distance* for seeing small details, such as ordinary type. This efficient distance is usually no closer than fifteen inches nor farther away than twenty inches from the eyes. The distances may change as we become older. The efficient distances are also longer for the few people who are farsighted but do not wear glasses to shorten the distance. And the distances are shorter for the few people who are nearsighted and do not wear glasses that lengthen their efficient focusing distances.

You can find your own particular effective distances for reading type by (1) closing your left eye and then (2) moving this page slowly toward your open right eye until the print just begins to look fuzzy or slightly indistinct—that is your near point for this size type. (3) Then move the page slowly away from you, in a straight line, until the words just begin to blur again—that is your far point. Near point and far point are usually five to six inches apart. (4) Now do the same with the other eye; if its focusing distance is not the same you may need glasses so both eyes focus at the same distance.

Halfway between the far point and the near point is your distance for most efficient seeing of objects this size. That is the distance at which you should be reading this. An inch or two one way or the other makes the eyes work a trifle harder to focus on the print.

People are usually careless about using their most efficient seeing distance, and are thus unfair to their eyes. To illustrate, when a short person sits at a desk, the letter lying on the desk top is likely to be too close, while for a tall person it is too far away. Or a person holds a magazine at a distance determined by the arms of the chair on which his elbows rest, rather than at the distance that gives him the clearest seeing.

Whenever you are going to use your eyes at a task for some time, test for the most efficient distance for that size object, and then arrange materials so you will look at it from that distance.

III

While trying to read that newspaper as it was lying flat on the table you could not obtain the most efficient distance. As your eyes moved down a column they had to keep changing their focus almost line by line, thus overworking the tiny ring of involuntary muscles that focus the lens of the eye—"eyestrain" may be one reward for this carelessness. In addition, that flat position of reading matter made you look downward—too much "neck strain," which is the typists' complaint when they lay the copy flat on the desk beside the typewriter.

Nor is that all. Part of the flat newspaper was beyond your far point of seeing, part closer than your near point—out of bounds, so to speak. It was the paragraphs that were out of bounds that you read inaccurately—371 Canal Street might be read 871 Carol Street, for instance—because things are fuzzy when they are out of bounds, no matter how much effort you make trying to get them to clear up.

Always tilt the page, or letter, or whatever you are reading so that the top of the page is the same distance from your eyes as the bottom

23. A TABLE EASEL FOR READING EFFICIENCY

A reading easel can hold what you are reading at an angle so that the page focuses at the same distance from top to bottom. It also leaves hands free for writing notes. This easel can be folded to carry and can be tilted to three positions. (Courtesy Endolane Enterprises, Antioch, Illinois)

of the page. In that position your eyes will not have to shift their focus appreciably from top to bottom. There is also less chance that glare from glossy paper will reflect light into your eyes.

The desks Thomas Jefferson designed had adjustable tops which could be tilted to an *efficient reading angle*. Some university and public libraries have table-top reading easels in their reading rooms to hold books at a more efficient reading angle; all libraries should have these. Office supply stores can secure similar book easels, or a handyman can easily make them. Tilt-top bedside tables can also be used as chair-side tables to hold books and magazines at efficient reading angles.

Dr. Vance T. Littlejohn, of the Woman's College of the University of North Carolina, tested the effect of tilted copyholders for typists. There was most fatigue when the copy was flat on the desk, least when the copy was tilted at an angle of 41 degrees to the desk top.

24. A WINDOW EASEL FOR READING EFFICIENCY

A homemade reading easel which swings from the window sill to adjust for the efficient seeing distance. The easel can be adjusted so that the pages of the book receive natural daylight without reflecting glare into the reader's eyes. Note the pencil and note paper prepositioned on the back of the easel.

An executive who has many letters to read should hold them at about that angle, or have a stand that holds them in that position so his hands are free. The housewife can prop the recipe book at an angle; maybe it will improve her cake.

The reading stands that are usually provided for public speakers and churches do not have enough tilt to be most efficient. Their tilt is usually cut down so as not to hide the speaker's face, so some of the reading matter is blurry as a consequence.

IV

The efficient focusing distance should also be considered when arranging workplaces and working materials. The ordinary file drawer, which is about twenty-seven inches deep, can be taken as an example.

A file clerk, standing at the front of the top drawer when it is open, will not be able to focus at all efficiently on the folders in the rear half of the drawer. She will have to bend over, if she is tall enough, or stand at the side of the open drawer, to read the rear half. Full-time file clerks soon learn to stand at the side of the drawers when thumbing through the folders.

In arranging work materials on a desk or assembly bench, the parts which will require close seeing should be nearest to the worker. The housewife should have the recipe she is trying out propped up at the front, not back, of the kitchen bench. The executive keeps his appointment schedule at the near edge of his desk, not only because it is easier to read there, but he is also less likely to forget to look at it.

Reading in bed has the approval of authorities, provided it is done under favorable conditions. The lighting should be favorable—and usually it isn't. The neck and shoulders should not be twisted—and usually they are. The reading material should be at an efficient focusing distance and at an efficient reading angle—usually it is not.

Don't snuggle down in a position for going to sleep and then try to read. Instead, prop yourself up with pillows or a back rest so your neck and shoulders will be comfortable, and so you can hold the book or magazine at the correct distance and angle for efficient seeing. And make sure that the lighting is adequate. Then read all you want to in bed.

V

The smaller the detail to be seen, the closer it should be to the eyes, but there is a limit to how close as we shall learn presently.

Letters typed in elite-size type need to be held an inch closer to be seen as clearly as those in the larger pica type. When footnotes or quotations are printed in smaller type than the main text, the book should be moved closer to read the smaller type—but remember to move it back as soon as you return to the larger type.

There are some occupations, and occasional tasks, which require one to look at very small details. It is usually foolish as well as inefficient to attempt seeing these with the naked eye. Most diemakers, for example, carry magnifying lenses to use when looking at fine markings. Most of the mirrors the dentist pokes into your mouth magnify the view for him.

There are times every week when most office workers could use a small hand lens to advantage, and there should be one as standard equipment in each desk. Strangely, some people hesitate to use a lens because they imagine it would indicate a weakness; the real weakness is in not having enough good sense to use one when it would be helpful.

When fine details have to be worked with most of the day it is often desirable while at work to wear eyeglasses that magnify slightly, even though eyes are perfectly normal. In one hosiery factory the girls who did the delicate work of completing the toes of sheer stockings were given such glasses to wear at work; as a result their output increased 15 per cent and their eyes no longer ached at the end of the day. Many surgeons wear weak magnifying glasses while operating.

VI

When looking for small details—threading a needle, deciphering the date on an old coin—it is essential to look squarely at the object. This is because a pinhead-size pit in the center of the retina is where details and colors are detected most accurately. If the image of the needle is focused slightly to one side of this central pit, it will be seen indistinctly.

Demonstrate this to yourself by looking sharply and steadily at a letter in the middle of the next line. The words at each side of the letter will be fuzzy and you will have difficulty reading them if you keep your eyes fixed squarely on the middle letter of the line.

Whatever you want to see clearly should be in a position so that a straight *fixation line* could be drawn from it through the center of the pupil and to the sensitive central pit. It is impossible to see either shape or color accurately out of the corner of your eye—the corner specializes in sensing motion and grays. More about motion shortly.

If the detail cannot be discerned when the object is a foot from the eye, there is no use getting closer to it, unless you happen to be very nearsighted, for the focusing power of the eye gives out at closer distances. (This is said to be the reason why people close their eyes when kissing.)

Use only one eye and a magnifying lens when objects have to be examined at less than a foot from the eye. If you try to use both eyes, you will make yourself temporarily cross-eyed, and in addition the image will not fall on the fixation line for one or perhaps both of your eyes. You may have noticed that watch repairmen use the magnifying lens on only one eye.

VII

When using only one eye your perception of depth is very inaccurate. Demonstrate this to yourself by closing one eye and then try to stick your left little finger through the dangling ring on a window-shade pull cord without touching the ring. It is easy when you use both eyes, but with one eye you will either miss the ring entirely, or set it spinning.

On those rare occasions when you have to use only one eye, be especially careful when you try to touch the object with your hands or some tool. Distance, or depth, cannot be seen accurately then and you have to "feel your way." You may have observed that the watch repairman steadies the heel of his hand on a hand rest of some sort and then carefully feels with the tool to touch the part he is looking at with one eye.

A few people have such poor vision in one eye that their perceptions of depth are generally erratic. They consequently are at a disadvantage when driving an automobile, especially when parking and turning corners or passing. If you knock things over at the dinner table, it may be for this reason.

VIII

The light should be brighter than customary when you want to see small details—the smaller the detail, the more light is needed. The amount of light needed on the following objects to make them equally visible is an illustration:

Ordinary book printed in 8-point type	10 foot-candles
Newspaper text	30 " "
Stock-market quotations in newspaper	100 " "
Seeing 1/64-inch markings on a steel rule	190 " "

How much light one needs depends also upon the color of the objects—100 foot-candles when sewing with white thread on white cloth, but 400 foot-candles for the same visibility if both thread and cloth are black.

The contrast between the object and its background also influences the efficiency of seeing. It is easier to read your penciled memo if it is on white paper than if on grayish paper, easier to see tiny screws if they are spread on dull (not glossy) white paper rather than on the dingy-colored bench top. More light is needed for reading a newspaper than a book because the newspaper is grayish, the book whiter.

Excessive contrast between the object and its background should be avoided, however, if it is to be looked at more or less continuously. White letterheads on a dark-colored desk, for example, make too much of a contrast to be easy on eyes. An ivory, very light gray, cream, or dull off-white desk top makes less contrast with the usual papers. The rule is to try to have the entire visual field about the same, without contrasting areas of light and dark.

Students often use large blotters covered with advertisements on the tops of their study tables. These blotters are usually of a dark-green color which makes too much contrast with the white pages of the books studied on them.

Much easier on the eyes is the system used by one banker. Each morning his secretary covers his entire desk top with a fresh sheet of dull white paper. During the day he does his scratch-pad figuring on this covering. If a dull white desk covering is too bright, it is because you are using direct lighting over it; the covering is efficient, the lighting is not. Change to indirect lighting and you will be better off in other ways, too.

8. Aids for Efficient Seeing

I

STAND AT AN EFFICIENT SEEING DISTANCE FROM A MIRROR TO LOOK at the pupils of your eyes. Then watch the pupils intently as you move your eyes to one side, then the other. You can't see them move, because eyes are as good as blind when they are moving. Eyes have to stay put in one position for a fraction of a second if we are to see any details. That is why chickens move their heads backward and forward while they are walking; their eyes can thus stay put long enough to distinguish details of possible food morsels.

This characteristic of our eyes makes them inefficient and also strains them when we (a) watch moving objects, or (b) move our eyes much while at work. This may be one reason why the assembly-line belt usually seems to be moving too fast for comfort.

Over-all efficiency, as well as seeing efficiency, can usually be greatly improved if you arrange work materials and equipment so that the eyes have to move as little as possible. The ideal would be to do eye work within an area the size of a dinner plate and at a distance of your most efficient seeing.

When two columns of figures are to be checked, for instance, move the columns side by side. Then the movement of the eyes will be shorter, and the focus will not have to shift when moving from one column to the other. This illustrates the principle of bringing the materials closer together and in the same focal plane whenever possible.

An oversize desk or workbench is an invitation to spread out work equipment so that that principle is violated. A smaller desk or bench forces a compact arrangement in a more efficient seeing area.

II

Many eye movements can be eliminated by *pre-positioning* equipment and materials. The radio repairman saves eye movements by keeping his soldering iron and solder always in the same location, and positioned so that he can (a) pick them up without looking at them, and (b) in a position so they are ready for use when they are picked up. No looking, no fumbling. So he doesn't lose sight of the place he wants to solder by having to look for the end of the iron to grasp.

Pre-positioning is a principle that has wide application, but is all too commonly neglected. The most-used articles in an office desk should be pre-positioned so that a paper clip, red pencil, or what not can be picked up correctly, ready to use, without having to move the eyes from other work.

The most-used articles in the kitchen should also be pre-positioned —the sharp-edged knives arranged from small to large with their handles toward the front of the drawer, cutting edge down; the salt and pepper in standard locations, and the salt larger than the pepper so you can tell which is which without having to look. Thus the eyes do not have to move and search for what is wanted.

III

Don't look at your hands unless it is unavoidable is a related principle. And you can be sure you do not have to watch them nearly so much as you do. The muscles of hands and fingers are well supplied with their own guiding senses. So are all voluntary muscles. Once a muscle group is trained for a task, it can usually do very well without being watched. Consider the typist, or violinist, or most any skilled workman; they go by "the feel" from their muscles, not by keeping watch with their eyes.

If a skilled typist or violinist tries to watch her fingers—a hunt-and-peck weakness—she becomes as muddled as the centipede that could not walk when it tried to see which foot it put forward first.

Once you try, you may be amazed how many things you can do guided mostly by muscles, with no need to move your eyes from their main work. You should write your signature without watching your fingers do it; other handwriting usually requires a little eye supervision. You can take the top off the toothpaste tube without looking—and with only one hand, but better look when you squeeze out the paste. You should button your clothes by feel, not by eyes. You should be

25. USE OTHER SENSES TO SPARE YOUR EYES

The blind do not have more sensitive fingers, but they do learn to make more skilled use of the senses in their skin and muscles. This blind worker is using an electronic gauge to inspect bearings for accuracy. For seeing workers the gauge flashes a light; for the blind it uses a loudspeaker. (Courtesy Timken Roller Bearing Company)

able to set the automobile handbrake, select speeds, switch on windshield wipers, sound the horn (only when necessary, we hope), and do the other essential driving operations without taking your eyes off traffic—or give up driving before you add to the accident statistics.

Your muscles are not nearly so helpless as to require all the eye supervision you give their movements. They do need some eye guidance when you drive a nail, thread a needle, or put on lipstick, but during much of your playtime and work time your eyes should be tending to their own business and should not interfere with what the muscles can do unaided. In this respect we have made ourselves more helpless than the blind.

Reduce your eye movements by having compact working areas, keeping equipment pre-positioned, and learning to do more things without using your eyes.

IV

There are some marked differences between people in the way their eyes can see, and these differences may have important effects upon personal efficiency. Fortunately, most of these individual eye differences can easily be modified by suitable eyeglasses. These are differences between people, not defects, any more than it is a defect to have big feet or small feet, or to have blue eyes rather than black. They are simply individual differences owing as a rule to the size and shape of the eyeball the person happens to have.

People whose eyeballs are slightly longer than average from front to back tend to be *shortsighted.* Objects have to be held close to their eyes so that the rays can be focused on the central pit. Jack Dempsey, heavyweight champion, and Marie Antoinette, glamorous queen of France, were among the famous who were nearsighted. W. K. Kellogg, the corn-flakes king, had trouble learning to read in school, and it was not until twenty years later that he found it was because of being so nearsighted he could scarcely see details. (It is not true, as baseball players often assert, that all umpires are nearsighted.)

In contrast, people with short eyeballs are *farsighted.* They can see far objects clearly but have to hold a letter at arm's length in order to read it. After about age forty more and more people become farsighted, which sometimes makes them clumsy when reaching for objects near them.

Sometimes the individual difference is in the curvature of the front parts of the eyes which may produce blurring in areas, similar to cheap window glass. This blurring in areas is called *astigmatism.* One eye may produce astigmatic blurring of up-and-down lines, while the other eye blurs the crosswise lines, or not at all. Just as sometimes, though rarely, a person's left eye may be nearsighted, the other farsighted.

Because our bodies keep on growing, or settling down, year after year, these differences usually change steadily through life. Eye shape keeps changing just as the waistline does; the change in waistline may be more obvious, but the change in eye shape may have more bearing on personal efficiency. People who were slightly nearsighted in childhood may grow into farsighted adults. Or people who had so-called perfect vision in their twenties may need glasses ten years later.

26. A TEST FOR ASTIGMATISM

Look at these, one eye at a time. If an eye has astigmatism one circle will appear blacker than the others. (Courtesy, Bausch and Lomb)

The records show that one person out of four in their twenties needs eyeglasses to make his seeing efficient. By age fifty one person out of two needs eyeglasses.

Thus regular eye tests are essential for the person who wishes to be efficient. These should be made on a regular schedule, once a year, whether the person feels "eyestrain" or not. The eyes change so gradually in most instances that the person does not become aware of the need until his eyes are really distressing him; he probably needed glasses a year or two before he became aware of this handicap to his efficiency.

Some companies have medical departments which make eye tests without charge to employees; some of these will also provide eyeglasses at wholesale cost. Even if you have to pay the full cost yourself, it is an investment in personal efficiency to have an annual eye test on your birthday—on your birthday so you will be more likely to remember to have the tests made.

And when you do wear glasses, form the habit of cleaning them every time you wash your hands. They can become dirty quicker than a nose becomes shiny. You never realize how much dust and grime float around in the air until you wear glasses.

Give yourself a birthday present of a complete eye examination.

V

There are some simple exercises which are considered helpful for more efficient use of the eyes. These are especially useful for the person who has used his eyes for an hour or so looking downward and at objects closer than arm's length. These exercises aim to give some relief not only to eye muscles but also to the neck muscles.

These exercises will not take the place of eyeglasses, if you happen to need them. Nor will they help you see more efficiently if the lighting is inadequate, or if you are trying to read the newspaper when it is flat on the desk. But they do provide relief and in addition seem to provide some resistance to future strain.

The person who looks downward and at less than arm's length at work should look into the far distance for a few moments once an hour. Look out the window at the most distant object you can locate, but not into the bright sun—and not when the boss is watching you. If there is no window, or if a nearby building blocks a distant view, then close your eyes for a few moments; they will roll upward naturally when closed. The coffee break is a good time to look into the distance instead of at the coffee cup or a magazine.

Typists, operators of business machines, and all others who look downward while working need to exercise their neck muscles, too. While looking into the distance, move the head from side to side, then up and down. Slowly. And as far as it will move without discomfort. It may also help to form the habit of holding your chin a bit higher in the air when you walk—but don't stumble at the curb.

When riding on trains or busses, look into the distance. Do not try to read anything smaller than newspaper headlines when riding (there is too much jiggling, bouncing, eye movement), and do not keep your eye on the moving traffic beside you (motion is very tiring to the eyes). Just look far ahead and upward; relax, daydream, or plan instead of trying to see.

In some occupations work can be arranged so that after an hour of close eye work the worker can switch to tasks which allow him to exercise his eyes by looking at things that are at more than arm's length. Do close-up work at the desk for an hour, then make phone calls or run errands. Sew for an hour, then vacuum, clean or make the beds.

When extra close eye work has to be done it is smart to spend a few minutes each day rotating the eyeballs. Close the eyes, then move them in a large circle, clockwise. Slowly. Then the same movement in the opposite direction. Move them a few times as far as they will go up and down; then right to left and back again.

Look up and into the distance from time to time; rotate your eyes, and limber up your neck. Pre-position your working equipment and materials, don't watch your hands any more than absolutely necessary while they are working, and give yourself that birthday present.

9. How Air Influences Your Efficiency

I

CLIMATE, WEATHER, VENTILATION, AIR CONDITIONING, ALL THESE DO much more than affect our comfort. The air around us affects our will-to-work, and in some extreme instances may make work impossible. When the atmosphere is favorable, we feel strong, alert. When unfavorable, it is difficult to concentrate, work drags, a feeling of dullness takes hold of us, and it is often impossible to use our capacities to their fullest.

And as the seasons roll around our efficiency often changes with the season. During the "summer slump," for example, most employers expect work to slow down and quality to be lowered. But this slump can often be greatly reduced—even eliminated—as will shortly be apparent.

The most obvious influence of the air around us is on muscular work. But the air also influences work done by bank clerks, students of mathematics, and other sedentary occupations. As the temperature goes up, for instance, Dr. Ellsworth Huntington, famous geographer and climatologist, found that bank clerks' bookkeeping errors were multiplied. And Dr. Raymond B. Cattell has found that people are more distractible in hot weather—it's harder to keep their minds on what they are doing, hence more errors and accidents.

Natural differences in climate and weather make some places more favorable than others for efficient working and living. Regions that tend to be hot, humid, with little air movement, greatly lower working efficiency. Cold does not have so much adverse influence, for reasons we come to in a moment. Prolonged winds are hard on efficiency; the summer wind in eastern Iran that blows violently from the north for four months without letting up, for example.

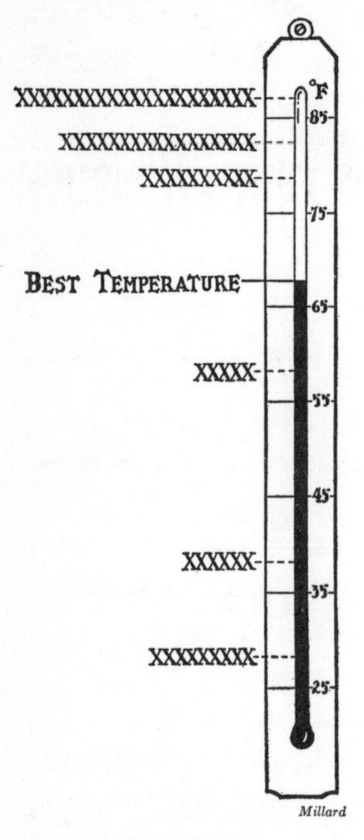

27. BOOKKEEPING ERRORS MADE BY BANK CLERKS

How the mistakes (X) made by bank clerks were influenced by the temperature. (Data from Dr. Ellsworth Huntington)

Dr. Huntington rated various parts of the world on the favorableness of their climates for human working efficiency. Some of his maps are reproduced here; you can find maps for other parts of the world in his book *Principles of Human Geography.*

These maps should be taken seriously when considering factory locations. The individual, too, should size up the climate before deciding to move some distance to take a new job. The climate may be the razor's edge that makes the difference between success and failure.

Brasilia, the new capital of Brazil, is an example of a wholesale move to a more favorable working climate. Ever since 1891 Brazilians had considered moving the capital from seacoast Rio de Janeiro to an inland plateau where the average temperature was 69 degrees F. But the plateau was all but inaccessible and was occupied by wild animals until 1956, when modern machinery was flown in to begin the construction of the new city and capital.

After four years of furious construction a new modern capital city was dedicated with 120,000 persons living in it. More than five thousand miles of highways had to be built to connect Brasilia with other cities, and the total cost reached $500,000,000 by the time the 2,333 truckloads of government records were moved to the more favorable climate.

But such a large-scale move is not always necessary to get a more favorable working climate. Air conditioning, for instance, can make the indoor climate efficient any place in the world. Yet we need to know how to get along in outdoor climate with least injury to health and efficiency, unless we plan to live cooped up indoors. And even if we live in a region where the climate is most favorable for personal efficiency, there are passing weather conditions that are handicapping.

II

How can climate, or weather, have such pervading effects on personal efficiency? It is essential to understand why, since most people's ideas about "good" or "bad" air have led them to do many things about it that are as useful as a parachute on a submarine.

The air we breathe, for one example, seldom has any effect on efficiency. We almost never need to worry about the air we breathe unless it happens to be loaded with smog or dusty chemicals, and that rarely happens.

But we do need to be careful every hour of the day about the qualities of the air that surrounds our bodies.

For centuries people—including ancient physicians—thought ventilation was needed to get rid of poisons it was imagined people gave off. A name was even dreamed up for this so-called poison—anthropotoxin. Yet no one had seen it, or been able to catch any in a bottle. "You don't need to see it," they said, "because when people are in an unventilated room for some time you can smell the anthropotoxin, and that is what makes the room stuffy. It causes headaches and

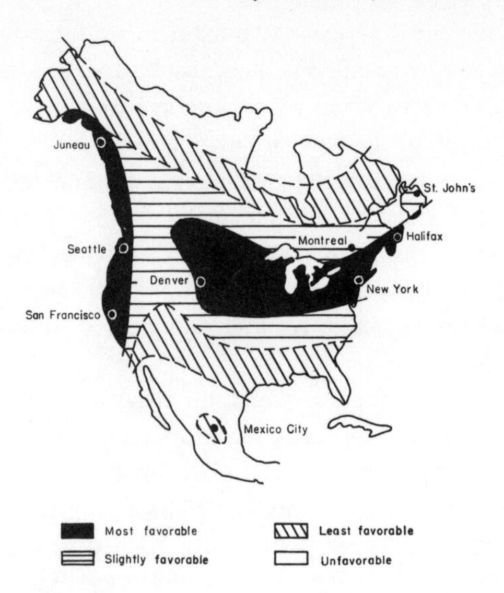

28. CLIMATIC EFFICIENCY IN NORTH AMERICA

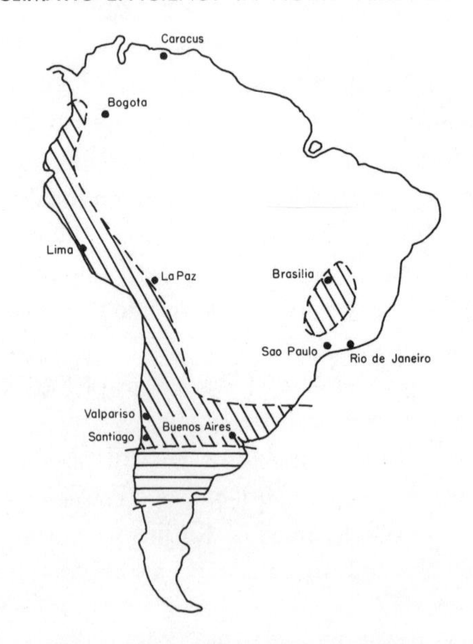

29. CLIMATIC EFFICIENCY IN SOUTH AMERICA

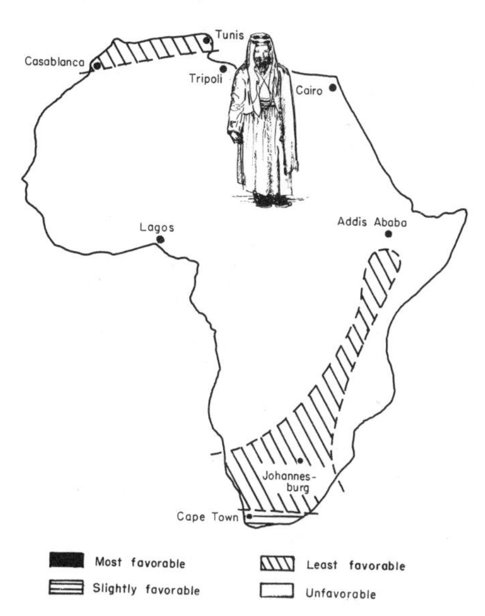

30. CLIMATIC EFFICIENCY IN AFRICA

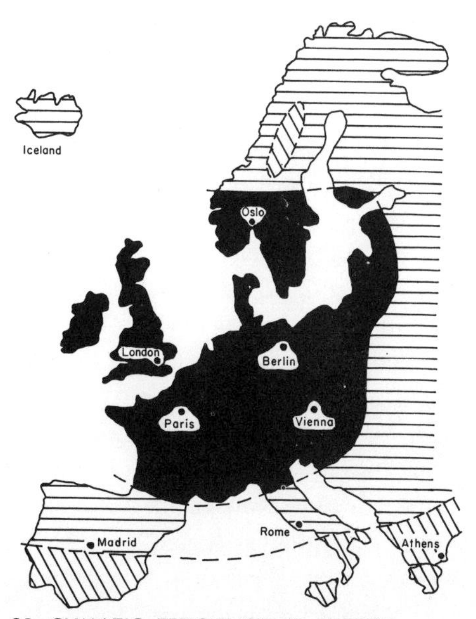

31. CLIMATIC EFFICIENCY IN EUROPE

makes people uncomfortable so that they can no longer work unless the windows are opened to let the poison out." That was the prevailing belief until . . .

Then a chemist, Antoine Lavoisier, who started work at six every morning to get more done, did catch something in a bottle. While Americans were fighting the Revolutionary War, Lavoisier developed new methods to analyze the air in rooms in Paris. He discovered that fresh outdoor air had only about 0.03 per cent of carbon dioxide, but that in a closed room occupied by people the carbon dioxide would rise to as much as 0.5 per cent.

From that discovery until World War I many scientists and most other people were convinced that we should ventilate in order to let the carbon dioxide out of the room. To be certain of having a good supply of pure air, people who could afford it built houses with high ceilings, and open-air porches for sleeping. Some became fresh-air fiends and made nuisances of themselves opening windows other people wanted closed.

Carbon dioxide is a fact, not a mere name as was anthropotoxin. But as far as efficiency goes, they have about equal importance.

III

It was not until early this century that Dr. Karl Flügge and three colleagues conducted some dramatic experiments which turned the prevailing ideas about "fresh air" topsy-turvy. These really simple experiments are classics in the development of modern science.

An airtight box was constructed in the laboratory of the Institute of Hygiene, of which Dr. Flügge was director, at the University of Breslau. The box was a little more than twice as large as a telephone booth. There was room enough in it for a person to move and work at the weight-lifting and mental tasks they experimented with, yet it was compact enough for the air in it to become contaminated within a few hours, if there were contaminants given off by humans at work.

After the average man had worked in this sealed box, breathing the same air over and over for four hours, the carbon dioxide inside the box would be as much as 1.5 per cent. But as long as the temperature and humidity inside the box were kept down, the men did not feel uncomfortable and did the work just as well as ever. They were comfortable, and working efficiently, despite the 1.5 per cent carbon dioxide they were breathing.

To make the test more severe, a man was next put in the airtight box for five hours. The carbon dioxide rose to 1.2 per cent and he had no complaints. Then they raised the temperature inside the box to 75 degrees F., and increased the humidity to 89 per cent. That ruined his day. He became very uncomfortable, and his work deteriorated. Perhaps it was not the carbon dioxide, but temperature and humidity, so the experimenters tried something different to find out.

This time they raised the temperature inside the box to 86 degrees F. and the relative humidity to 87 per cent—hot and muggy inside. The carbon dioxide slowly rose to 1.1 per cent. Soon the man felt he couldn't stand it any longer, so put on a breathing mask which was connected to the outside, and he could thus breathe fresh air although his body was still surrounded by the muggy heat. But breathing that fresh air did not give him any relief.

The poor fellow felt fine, however, a few moments after they lowered the temperature inside the box to 63 degrees F., although by this time the carbon dioxide he was breathing was 1.6 per cent.

Every such critical test showed that the men were scarcely affected by the air they breathed into their lungs. But invariably their efficiency and comfort were lowered when their bodies were surrounded by hot, moist, motionless air.

Those experiments at the Institute of Hygiene revolutionized our notions about good working air and ventilation. Other scientists quickly made similar tests, and their results confirmed the conclusion that it is the air around our skins rather than in our lungs that ordinarily has important effects upon efficiency, comfort, and general well-being.

IV

Why does the air around our skins affect our efficiency?

Chiefly because where there is human life there is heat. The chemical processes of living produce body heat steadily, even when we are not working. The average adult who is "just sitting" gives off some 400 B.T.U. (British Thermal Units, one of which is enough heat to raise one pound of water 1 degree F.) of heat each hour—enough

B.T.U. to boil a quart of water. Several people watching the same television set will warm up a small room by their own body heat.

We keep on making body heat, day and night, until we die. We have to lose as much surplus heat as we produce to keep the body in an efficient, steady state. If you were unable to give off that heat while just sitting, your body temperature would rise 3 degrees F. in one hour—to fever temperature.

As soon as physical work is done, the heat that is produced in the body is boosted upward. When you get up from just sitting and climb the stairs, your heat production hurdles up at the rate of 2,000 B.T.U. per hour—enough heat to boil a gallon of water. Dr. Walter B. Cannon, Harvard physiologist, told scientists that twenty minutes of the hardest muscular work produced enough heat to cook the albumen in the body like a hard-boiled egg, unless the heat were dissipated into the surrounding air. That almost happens in cases of heat exhaustion or sunstroke, about which more shortly.

Most of the time we are able to lose the surplus body heat without such dire results. But some climatic or weather or working conditions make it difficult to lose the body heat rapidly enough, and then the body's steady state is thrown off balance. It may also stay off balance for some time after the weather has improved. After a long, hot spell, for instance, people seldom snap back into an efficient condition as soon as the weather becomes comfortable again; it may take a week or longer to recover from the lingering effects.

V

How do we lose this surplus body heat? And what can we do to lose it promptly before our efficiency suffers?

We have our own personal cooling system. When we understand this system's amazing operations we have the keys that unlock the doors to greater efficiency in unfavorable weather and climates—no worries then about becoming hard-boiled eggs.

Most of the surplus heat is lost from your skin. The capillaries in the skin dilate, allowing more blood than usual to flow near the surface where it can give off heat more readily. This shift of blood flow to the skin is really enormous. Dr. Alan E. Burton measured the shift in fingers and found it not at all unusual for their blood flow to be increased by one hundred times. When the legs were warmed for thirty minutes by a heat pad, for instance, the blood flow in the fingers (which were not heated directly) increased by eighty or more times. In his tests he also had one man live for several days in a room where the temperature was ninety degrees F. and the air damp and humid. After five days the blood flow in his fingers was more than one hundred times what it had been in ordinary room temperatures.

With such a great shift of blood to the skin as a starter, here is the way the surplus heat is taken away when you are doing sedentary work in an ordinary room and wearing comfortable clothing:

About 45 per cent of your surplus heat is lost by simple *radiation* from the skin. Some of the radiated heat is absorbed by the desk you are working at, the wall behind you, the floor under you. Sometimes the nearby objects are warmer than you are, in which case they do not absorb any of your excess heat but instead radiate their heat to you. If a hot-water pipe runs under the floor where you sit, you may absorb rather than radiate. Or if you use a desk lamp with an incandescent bulb it will be hotter than you are—better change to a fluorescent desk light, for the hot months at least.

Another 25 per cent of that surplus heat is lost through *convection* and *conduction*. Dr. Guy P. Crowden reported to the Royal Institute of Public Health and Hygiene that one person gives off enough heat by convection and conduction during an hour of just sitting to raise the temperature of a 9 by 9 foot bathroom by 10 degrees F.

So the chair you are sitting on becomes warm from heat conducted from your body. The tools you hold in your hands, also.

Convection accounts for a larger share of the loss of surplus heat. Moving air particles convey the air away, provided there is some air movement. A blowing fan increases the convection. Holding an iced soda-pop bottle in your hand increases the conduction.

While doing sedentary work there is another 15 per cent of surplus heat lost by *evaporation* of moisture from the skin. You may not be aware that you are perspiring at light work, but there is so-called insensible perspiration all the time. We usually do not become aware of it because it evaporates quickly and does not collect into "beads of sweat."

As this insensible perspiration evaporates, it absorbs heat from the skin and thus cools it slightly, the same way that rubbing alcohol cools as it evaporates from your hand. There is less evaporation when the room air is humid, in which case you may begin to feel uncomfortable and less efficient. There is less evaporation, also, if the air is motionless.

About 8 per cent more of your surplus heat is dissipated into the surrounding air by *vaporization* of water from your lungs. The air you breathe out is saturated with moisture, as you can see on a frosty morning when the moisture freezes in the cold air a few inches from your nostrils.

The remainder of the surplus is lost in such relatively minor ways as warming up the air that is breathed in, carbon dioxide emerging from solution in the lungs, and by the body wastes.

It is really a wonderful cooling system we have, and the details we have outlined have very practical applications we will take up in the following chapters. Physiologists sum up these methods of keeping the body efficient in hot weather by facetiously advising people to sit naked under a tree with their feet dangling in a cool spring.

We can become slightly acclimatized to hot weather after we have been in it for about a week, but the records indicate that we have to take some active exercise during this period if the body is to adjust to the heat. The first week of a hot spell would thus be the worst week, provided the person was physically active during that first week. People doing manual work would be more likely to become acclimatized than the white-collar office worker.

VI

When the surplus heat is not lost rapidly enough people begin to feel uncomfortable and do not want to work. They may get prickly heat—itching and tiny blisters in their skin—even if they do no work.

If the surplus heat accumulates, as it does when we do heavy physical work in hot, humid air, the person becomes unable to work because his body soon stalls.

For efficient work—whether heavy or light—the air around you has to be favorable for radiating, convecting, conducting, and evaporating your surplus heat. Even when you are doing nothing more strenuous than just sitting, or trying to sleep.

To be favorable for personal efficiency, the air around you has to have sufficient cooling power to take away the surplus. The cooling power depends upon three characteristics of the air: temperature, relative humidity, and movement.

Rarely does the surrounding air have too much cooling power. The problem for most people, in most places on earth, and for much of the year, is to manage somehow to get more cooling power. It is a problem most of the year in the regions in the unfavorable zones on the maps, but it is also a problem for a few months even in the most favorable zones.

10. How to Have an Efficient Working Temperature

I

WHAT ROOM TEMPERATURE IS THE MOST EFFICIENT FOR GETTING things done?

It depends partly upon air movement and humidity, which affect the cooling power of the air around you. It also depends upon how heavy or how sedentary your work is. A low temperature for example, has a more unfavorable influence on sedentary work than on strenuous muscular work; the muscular work produces much greater amounts of surplus body heat. Thus it is wise to save up some heavy work for colder days and sedentary work for hot days.

By and large, the temperature plays the major part in working efficiency. So we will first report the most favorable temperature conditions, and ways to make them more favorable; air movement and humidity will come later.

II

The most widely accepted standards for the "ideal temperature" come from thirty-five years of research by Professor Constantin P. Yaglou, of the Harvard School of Public Health. Considering the *feeling of comfort,* he found that United States women prefer a temperature of 72 degrees F. to 76 degrees F., while men prefer a temperature of 62 degrees F. to 72 degrees F. He also found that the average woman could stand summer heat better than men. (During the menopause, and in some thyroid disorders, women may be pestered by "hot flashes" and want it much cooler.)

Why do women prefer it warmer? Probably mostly because of the way they dress. Women wear thinner clothing, more of their skin area is exposed, and skirts permit more cooling circulation of air than men's trousers do.

In England the comfortable temperature is several degrees lower than in the United States, also probably because of clothes—women's as well as men's. The English wear much warmer clothing than is customary in the New World. This helps keep the fuel bill down during the winter months, and since English summers are not so hot as American the thicker clothing is not the summer handicap it would be in the United States.

Concerning *work output,* Professor Yaglou found that from a rather chilly 40 degrees F. up to 75 degrees F. room temperature did not have much effect. But output, especially for hard muscle work, begins to fall off after the temperature goes above 75 degrees F., and falls off rapidly after 80 degrees F.

Accidents increase as the temperature goes above the comfortable zone, more so for older than for younger people. As we might suspect now, high temperatures do not cause much increase in women's accidents.

Authorities agree that the *most favorable temperature* for work is from 68 degrees F. to 70 degrees F., and that around 75 degrees F. is the *critical temperature* above which efficiency and well-being are almost always lowered.

The most favorable temperature is lower than the balmy temperature people prefer on the basis of comfort alone. Since homes and workplaces are usually heated to give a feeling of comfort, they are a few degrees too warm for maximum efficiency. If the room were heated to a less balmy temperature, the occupants would more likely "get a move on" with their work.

Cold walls and cold floors lead people to prefer temperatures that are too balmy for greatest efficiency. When the outside wall is not insulated, it is colder than the rest of the room, producing a "drafty feeling," and a higher temperature is wanted for comfort. Also, when the temperature on the floor is 5 degrees F. lower than at head height, a higher temperature is preferred. If you have the heat distributed more uniformly throughout the room, a lower and more efficient temperature becomes comfortable.

During the warm months the temperature usually rises above the critical point of 75 degrees F. for days at a time, except near the polar regions. The two tables show the summer average and also the highest temperature for a few world capitals and for several United States cities. There are periods in every city on these lists when the temperature is so high it lowers personal efficiency seriously. In fact, it is difficult to find any inhabited place on the globe where there are not days when the temperature of working places needs to be lowered.

Everything possible should be done to keep the temperature where you work from going above 75 degrees F. during warm weather. In cold weather learn to be comfortable in 70 degrees F. heat.

RANKING OF SOME WORLD CITIES ON HOT-WEATHER TEMPERATURE
(Average of their Three Hot Months)

Most favorable for personal efficiency:

	Average	*Highest*
Amsterdam	62°F.	91°F.
Berlin	63	99
Brussels	62	97
Geneva	65	101
Leningrad	61	97
London	61	100
Mexico City	63	91
Moscow	63	100
Oslo	61	95
Paris	64	101
Quebec	64	97
Vancouver	63	92

Slightly favorable for personal efficiency:

	Average	*Highest*
Budapest	69°F.	99°F.
Cape Town	69	104
Lisbon	69	103
Melbourne	66	111
Montreal	67	97
Vienna	66	98

Least favorable for personal efficiency:

	Average	*Highest*
Buenos Aires	73°F.	104°F.
Istanbul	73	104
Madrid	73	112
Marseilles	70	100
Rome	75	108
Tokyo	74	98

Unfavorable for personal efficiency:

	Average	*Highest*
Athens	79°F.	109°F.
Bombay	80	100
Peiping	77	107
Rio de Janerio	77	102
Shanghai	78	103

RANKING OF SOME UNITED STATES CITIES ON HOT-WEATHER TEMPERATURE
(Average of the Three Hot Months)

Most favorable for personal efficiency:

	Average	*Highest*
Duluth, Minnesota	61°F.	106°F.
Helena, Montana	65	108
Lander, Wyoming	64	102
Northfield, Vermont	64	98
Portland, Oregon	65	105
Sault Ste. Marie, Michigan	62	98
Seattle, Washington	62	98

Slightly favorable for personal efficiency:

	Average	*Highest*
Bismarck, North Dakota	67°F.	114°F.
Boston, Massachusetts	69	104
Buffalo, New York	67	97
Green Bay, Wisconsin	67	104
Huron, South Dakota	68	111
Los Angeles, California	69	109
Rapid City, South Dakota	68	106
St. Paul, Minnesota	69	104
Santa Fe, New Mexico	67	97
Spokane, Washington	67	108

Least favorable for personal efficiency:

	Average	*Highest*
Albany, New York	70°F.	104°F.
Atlantic City, New Jersey	70	104
Chicago, Illinois	72	105
Cleveland, Ohio	70	100
Denver, Colorado	70	105
Des Moines, Iowa	73	110
Harrisburg, Pennsylvania	73	104
Indianapolis, Indiana	74	106
New York, New York	72	102
Omaha, Nebraska	74	114
Parkersburg, West Virginia	74	106
Philadelphia, Pennsylvania	74	106
Springfield, Illinois	74	110

Unfavorable for personal efficiency:

	Average	*Highest*
Atlanta, Georgia	77°F.	102°F.
Dodge City, Kansas	76	109
Fresno, California	79	115
Jacksonville, Florida	81	104
Kansas City, Missouri	76	113
Knoxville, Tennessee	76	104
Little Rock, Arkansas	79	108
Louisville, Kentucky	77	107
Lynchburg, Virginia	65	106
Montgomery, Alabama	80	107
New Orleans, Louisiana	81	102
Oklahoma City, Oklahoma	78	113
Phoenix, Arizona	87	119
St. Louis, Missouri	76	110
San Antonio, Texas	82	108
Springfield, Missouri	75	106
Tampa, Florida	81	98
Vicksburg, Mississippi	84	104
Washington, D.C.	77	103

III

How can you keep the temperature down to avoid hot-weather slump?

Air conditioning, of course, can keep the indoor temperature down within the comfort and efficiency zone. For example, I am writing this at 3:15 P.M. on an unseasonably hot early September day. The temperature in the shade just outside the window is 95 degrees F., the relative humidity is 54 per cent, scarcely a breath of air is stirring, and the pollen count is 175.

But indoors where I am doing sedentary work that produces some 400 B.T.U. of body heat an hour, the air temperature is only 75 degrees F., the relative humidity 37 per cent and the air is gently moving at around thirty feet per minute—air movement enough to waft pipe smoke slowly to the exhaust ducts but not enough to feel as a draft. The pollen count in the room is probably around zero because the air is cleaned day and night by an electrostatic precipitron that removes dust, pollens, yeast, and fungus spores, even pipe smoke. A day indoors that engineers have made wonderful for working, and the night will be wonderful for sleeping, despite the heat, humidity, and pollen outside.

Do I regret having to drive an old-model automobile and not having the latest fashions in clothes? Not when those savings provide nearly ideal atmospheric conditions for working or loafing inside the house! Not when school children were dismissed this morning, and city-hall and other office workers were given the day off because it was "too hot to work"—they are paying in inefficiency for the air conditioning they do not have.

Take a second thought before you accept work with a firm that does not have air conditioning where you will be working. You will find that some firms have air-conditioned rooms even for intrinsically hot jobs in smelters and foundries.

And when renting or building a house, think seriously about settling on one a little smaller if necessary in order to afford one that is fully air conditioned.

IV

There are numerous ways to keep the temperature lower when complete air conditioning is not possible. Self-management looms large in this. Many of the ways are also useful even if there is air conditioning. We will summarize these in seven groups.

1. *Keep out of the sun* when you work outside and the temperature

is above 80 degrees F. in the shade. Self-management. Protect yourself against the heat which radiates directly from the sun and is probably higher than your own body temperature. You cannot lose surplus heat when you are surrounded by air that is hotter than you are.

On very hot days plan your outside work so you can "follow the shade," even if it means working a few hours at dawn, or at dusk, and a siesta during the full heat of the day. Today, for instance, from 6:30 to 8:30 A.M. by which time the temperature was 82 degrees F. outside, I dug and chopped stump roots in the woods at the riverbank —and quit when I worked up some visible perspiration. Then I went to desk work in air-conditioned efficiency. After the evening meal I will cut grass for an hour, in the shade as well as the cool of the day; since it is lighter work than digging and chopping there will be only insensible perspiration.

In the wintertime I manage my life differently and do the outdoor work in early afternoon when it is warmest outside. (Except when overnight snow has to be cleared away the first thing in the morning.)

Sun bathing is unnecessary and potentially dangerous. The possible discomfort from sunburn is minor in view of what too much sun can do. The so-called "healthy tan," which sun bathers seek, is in fact undesirable because it makes the skin opaque to the beneficial rays in moderate sunlight. "Keep your shirt on" is good advice when working in the sun.

Fun in the sun can end in tragedy. A *sunstroke,* or heat prostration, may be caused by insolation (exposure to the rays of solar energy), due to the impossibility of getting rid of the surplus body heat. These strokes may merely prostrate the individual for a few days, but they may also damage nervous tissues and lead to death.

During the ten years from 1949 to 1958 there were 5,208 deaths from excessive heat and insolation in the United States. They occur even in the coldest and northernmost states. This is almost three times the number of deaths from lightning. Each of the deaths from excessive heat and insolation was unnecessary.

2. *Screen yourself from heat sources* for the same reasons you keep out of the sun on hot days. This is why the automobile engine is partitioned off from the passengers' section of the car body.

In one forge operation the temperature striking workers' faces was reduced 27 degrees F. by putting a sheet of heat-resistant glass between the workers and the forge. A screen of rigid asbestos between workers and the soldering irons they used reduced the temperature on their faces by 5 degrees F. In the kitchen, a portable folding screen of aluminum can be stood in front of the burner to shield the housewife from the radiant heat of the burner; it will also limit the spattering of grease.

3. *Keep the sun out* of buildings on hot days. Trees that shade both roof and side walls can make the temperature several degrees lower on the inside. The trees have to be tall, and as close to the building as the drainage tile allow. Bear that in mind in selecting a building site.

Wide overhanging eaves keep the sun off part of the side walls and sometimes shade the windows that are near the eaves, but they do not give the over-all protection that big shade trees—and plenty of them—do.

Use awnings on windows the sun strikes, even if there is an overhanging eave. White awnings, or natural aluminum color, with open rather than boxed ends, are coolest. Lower the awnings before the sun hits the windows.

If there are no awnings, pull the window shades. White shades are coolest and darken the room least.

Special "sunproof" aluminum screening, made with hundreds of tiny louvres, keeps the sun out effectively and lowers the indoor temperature. It also lowers the natural lighting.

If there are skylights, as in sawtooth factory-roof constructions, one might as well declare a holiday on hot days.

4. *Keep the heat out* by closing windows and doors *before* the outdoor temperature becomes higher than the indoor. Open them *after* the outside temperature falls below that indoors.

Use outside doors as little as possible during hot weather. If you have careless children or thoughtless adults, put an automatic door closer on outside doors.

When air conditioning is installed, it can be engineered so that the indoors is under a slight positive air pressure. In such cases the indoor pressure holds back the outside air and keeps outdoor heat from coming inside through cracks and open doors.

Thermal windows made of two layers of glass separated by an air space keep heat out. If you use an air conditioner, keep the storm windows on during hot weather to get the benefits of a double layer of glass.

Insulate the side walls and attic; don't skimp either on quality or amount.

Make your next roof a light-colored one, which will produce a cooler attic than does a dark roof. Side walls, too, are cooler when they are light colored on the outside.

Concrete or asphalt drives, walks, and patios reflect heat into the building. A swimming pool may, too. Screen their heat from the building by tall hedges. Or lower their heat by large trees which shade them.

5. *Reduce the sources of heat indoors.* Insulate hot-water pipes with at least an inch of rigid fiber glass. Use fluorescent rather than incandescent lights. Turn off the pilot lights on the stove and use matches instead. Cook in the back yard, or use foods that need little cooking.

If a heat source has to be used, blow its vagrant heat outdoors. An exhaust fan directly over the stove can reduce the heat around the stove by 20 degrees F. if the fan is vented to the outside. If there is no exhaust fan, close the kitchen doors when using the stove and open both the top and bottom of the window.

People themselves are sources of heat. The fewer people in a room, the cooler it will be. Also, the lighter the work they do, the less heat they add to the room. Postpone the heavy work until the weather moderates, and take advantage of the hot spell to read some useful book which will not increase your body heat production.

6. *Work where it is coolest in the building.* Rooms on the north side are usually cooler. The bottom floors are cooler than upper floors, unless a stove or operation that makes heat is on the lower floor.

The side of a room farthest from the window, or farthest from the outside wall, is usually cooler. You will generally lose more surplus heat by radiation if you work close to the inside (cooler) wall; you are more likely to feel stifling if beside the outside wall in the same room.

You can lose more surplus heat by conduction if you move to a cool chair from time to time. We knew a lovely elderly Quaker lady in Philadelphia who took advantage of conduction by spending the hottest hours in a bathtub partly filled with water where she crocheted and read books. "Better than the beach," she chirruped, "no sand in my crocheting, no flies in my hair, and no squealing youngsters splashing around."

7. *Cool off, but not too much, or too rapidly.* When the weather or hot working environment produces sweating, it is wise (a) to slow down your activity so the surplus body heat will not increase, and (b) get in a cooler place for a few moments. Foundry workers, for instance, rest in the cool end of the shop, or outdoors in the shade, or in front of a fan, between pouring heats of molten metal. Sometimes they douse their heads with cold water.

Cold water on the skin is very cooling—sometimes too cooling—because it is cold to begin with and because water conducts heat some fourteen times better than air does.

But a cold shower is not so cooling as it feels at the time. It cools the body surface so much that the body is stimulated to produce more heat! As a result, fifteen minutes after taking a cold shower you may be perspiring more than before. For a shower that has a lasting cooling effect the water should be lukewarm.

Standing close to a large fan may have a similar unexpected effect if it cools you too much and too rapidly.

Excessive drinking of iced beverages also stimulates the body to produce heat instead of remaining cooled. Authorities recommend slow sipping of iced drinks, holding the sip in the mouth a few moments before swallowing it. When very hot and very thirsty—they usually go together—it is more efficient to drink slightly cooled water, and slowly, rather than iced drinks.

If the cooling is too rapid, it may bring on heat cramps; spasms in muscles, painful muscles, and weakened heart action.

Some smelters and foundries have found it profitable to set up separate air-conditioned rooms in which workmen can rest between heats. The temperature in the workroom itself may reach as high as 110 degrees F. during hot weather, and be as low as 78 degrees F. in the winter. The air conditioning of the rest-pause room is adjusted according to the workroom temperature, in order to avoid too rapid cooling. The general practice is to have the cool room about 10 degrees F. cooler than the workroom.

Dr. Lucien A. Brouha found that after eight hours' work in a smelter the average worker who did not cool off in the cooled room had a body temperature of 99.7 degrees F. But the men who used the cooled room between pourings had body temperatures a degree lower at the end of the workday. And during their rest periods the men who rested in the cooled room had pulse rates of 78 beats per minute, much more favorable than the 85 beats of the men who rested elsewhere.

Do everything you can to keep the heat down to 75 degrees F., and to keep out of the heat, and watch the way you work and rest and cool off.

11. What to Do About Air Movement

I

"IT IS SO STIFLING IN HERE I CAN'T WORK." SUCH A REMARK MEANS it is time to push the air around. You are, so to speak, becalmed, or in the doldrums, which makes it difficult for you to use your capacities.

Get the air moving and it will dissipate some of your excess body heat. The temperature of the air will not be lowered by moving it, of course, but moving air conveys away more of the body heat and also helps us lose heat by evaporation of insensible perspiration. Soon after a breeze strikes you there is a feeling of relief—unless you are dressed so that air currents cannot reach your body surface.

How greatly air movement helps when the temperature soars was shown by Professor Constantin P. Yaglou's records. He found that most people feel comfortable and can work efficiently at sedentary work in a room temperature of 72 degrees F. with relative humidity of 30 per cent and the air standing still. But late in the forenoon, when the temperature rises to 75 degrees F. and nothing else changes, you will feel uncomfortable and your work will suffer.

But you will soon feel comfortable in spite of that 75 degrees F. temperature if the air is pushed around so that it moves about one-half mile an hour. That is so slight a movement that you cannot feel a breeze, and it will scarcely waft tobacco smoke. It is enough air movement, however, to waft more of the surplus heat from your body surface so that you are as comfortable as when becalmed in a 72 degrees F. temperature.

In the afternoon, if the room temperature goes up to 80 degrees F., you will feel exceedingly uncomfortable and be markedly inefficient if the air is becalmed. For that temperature the air movement will have to be speeded up to three miles an hour to make you feel comfortable again.

Will that three-miles-an-hour speed cause unpleasant drafts? No. It is about the speed of the average walk and can barely be felt on hands and face. It will waft smoke but not blow the papers on your desk. Nor will it be felt as a draft when the temperature is 80 degrees F., unless it is cold air or you happen to be sitting near a cold wall. It would feel like a draft, however, if the room temperature was down to 72 degrees F.; then you would want to roll down your sleeves and put on a coat.

(Air speed has to be from four to seven miles an hour to be classed as a light breeze. A speed of one to three miles is called light air, and when less than a mile per hour you are becalmed, or in the doldrums.)

When the temperature goes up to 75 degrees F., set the air in motion. The higher the temperature, or the heavier the work, the more air speed is needed for efficiency and comfort.

II

Can the natural outdoor breezes be used to move the air indoors?

In many regions the prevailing winds can provide efficiency-making comfort during moderately warm, but not hot, weather. The average wind speed in New York City and Buffalo is fourteen miles an hour—a moderate breeze. At Albuquerque, Chicago, Key West, and Philadelphia it is nine miles an hour—a gentle breeze. At Chattanooga, Knoxville, San Diego, and Washington, D.C., it is seven miles—a light breeze.

Ventilation through open doors and windows can bring a part of these natural air currents indoors where they can be of real benefit until the outdoor temperature climbs to 80 degrees F. When 80 degrees F. is reached outside, the heat brought in on the breeze will usually offset its cooling power.

Thus we need to modify the earlier rule about closing doors and windows before the outside temperature is 75 degrees F. On days when there is a light breeze blowing—strong enough to rustle leaves —and the weather forecast is for a high of not above 80 degrees F., leave the doors and windows open. But if the forecast is for a high of more than 80 degrees F., close them before the outside reaches 75 degrees F.

More movement of outside air indoors is possible when windows can be opened on opposite walls, allowing for cross ventilation. Pivoted or hinged windows that swing out at the bottom keep rain out, but they also keep the air out, unless they are tilted to a full horizontal position.

The famous old southern mansions had large hallways from front to back, with large doors at each end to give breezes clear sailing through the halls. These wide hallways were often used as sitting rooms during hot spells, not quite so cool as a cucumber but the coolest place in the house.

Window drapes and curtains restrict the flow of incoming breezes; pin them back. Louvered window screens impede the air flow seriously. So does tall furniture in the path of the air through the room.

III

The location of the building affects the natural air flow. If nearby buildings are too close, air movement is hampered. A large-scale example of this is Chicago, "The Windy City," which is no longer so windy because there are now big buildings close together which deflect the natural breezes. In cities the world over buildings are too close together for summer comfort.

Most localities have a prevailing wind direction, but it does not always come from the North Pole in winter and from the Equator in summer, as it may sometimes seem. In the North Temperate Zone the winds come principally from the west, but local hills, valleys, and obstacles may alter this. In positioning a building and its windows, the prevailing wind in that locality during the hot months should be considered. When the wind is mostly from the west, for illustration, a big barn to the west of the house would give the hay and livestock the natural breeze and divert it from the farm family.

The flow of air indoors is often impeded by barricades—as obstructing as that barn—which divert the breezes from where they would be of most benefit. The typist who is hemmed in by tall file cabinets is working in becalmed air. The executive who has an impressive desk with pedestals that hug the floor will find the lower half of his body becalmed. The person who works in a corner is likely to be almost as becalmed as if he were in a telephone booth; he should move out into the path of the air currents for the duration of the warm spell. Work at a table in preference to a knee-hole desk during warm weather. If the bed is in a corner, move it into the path of the air currents on hot nights.

Remove obstructions so that the natural air currents can have clear sailing.

IV

It is possible to create a natural breeze that will make homes and workplaces more efficient.

A large porch creates a breeze by the area of shade it makes. On a sunny day the shaded area will have a slightly lower temperature than the surrounding air, and this difference of temperature between two masses of air is often enough to set up a natural current in the immediate vicinity. A small porch does not have much of this effect. But a really large porch, with windows opening into the house from it, will add to the indoor comfort.

A grove of large trees beside a building is much more effective than a porch for creating a natural breeze, because it cools a larger mass of air. A few smallish trees scattered around the lot have little of this effect. A couple dozen really large trees so close together that their branches touch to form a solid area of shade—and the lower branches high enough for an adult to walk under—can produce conditions which start enough breeze to rustle the lower leaves. Open the windows nearest this grove and let the cooling breezes come in.

Thomas Jefferson took advantage of this type of natural breeze by using a poplar grove for his work during hot periods. (He had cleared out the underbrush so the breezes would not be obstructed.) The grove, unfortunately, was not close enough to the mansion for its breezes to give cooling power inside, so Jefferson went to the grove.

A large body of water near a building will also create a local breeze, because the water temperature is different from the air. This "lake breeze" is familiar to those who can afford a summer home on a lake. A sizable body of water is needed; a small pond or swimming pool is seldom sufficient. Rivers are usually too small, but if there are groves along their banks to give an assist, the combined results may be a comforting "river breeze." One drawback, however, is that under some weather conditions the nearby body of water may make the air too humid for efficient working.

Help nature help you get sufficient air movement.

32. JEFFERSON'S MONTICELLO

A large porch and large trees create conditions which can set up a cooling breeze in their vicinity. Monticello would have been several degrees cooler in hot weather if the trees had also shaded the roof from the midday sun. The roof of Jefferson's smaller house, Poplar Forest, was shaded all day and he went there to work during the hot weather. Both houses were designed and built by Jefferson, in the same style of architecture. (Courtesy the Thomas Jefferson Memorial Foundation, Inc.)

V

How can we get adequate air movement when there is no natural breeze? The answer is not quite so obvious as it may seem.

In hot oriental countries the indoor air was kept on the move by a punkah, a large cloth-covered frame hanging from the ceiling. The punkah was slowly pushed to and fro by a servant. The less well-to-do fanned themselves with palm-leaf fans or pieces of cardboard. Thomas A. Edison usually had a palm-leaf fan in his hand during hot spells. (He made the first successful electric lamp filament from the bamboo binding on his palm-leaf fan.)

At present electric fans can keep the air on the go. In one garment plant fans alone increased the cooling power of the air 40 per cent close to the fan and 10 per cent in the remote corners of the workroom.

There are a few fine points to note when using electric fans. First, use a fan of good quality. The motor in a cheap fan is likely to give off much more heat; some cheap fan motors get too hot to touch. The motor should feel only slightly warm to the touch after being used an hour.

The fan should have three speeds, to give slight air movement when the temperature is 75 degrees F., and greater speed when the room is hotter and more air motion is required for comfort.

Give preference to a quiet fan, and a large one is usually quieter. A big fan running at low speed will move more air, and with less noise, than a little fellow whirring at top speed.

The fan should oscillate back and forth so that the air is stirred throughout the room rather than in a one-way current, thus preventing "dead corners." In addition, the air feels fresher, less stifling, when its speed is variable.

Direct the fan so that there is sufficient air movement on the person. The fan does not cool the wall or room air; it may actually heat them if it has a hot motor or if it sucks in hot outside air from an open window. It cools only because it facilitates the loss of surplus body heat by convection and evaporation.

When there is more than one person working in a room, an oscillating fan may cover them adequately, or extra fans may be needed, or the workplaces may have to be moved closer together so that each person gets some cooling air movement.

If the natural air movement is not sufficiently cooling, give the air a push and keep pushing it until the weather changes.

(Occasionally a factory worker tries to cool himself with a blast of compressed air from the air hose. If he is able to stand some ten feet from the nozzle, it may benefit him. But if he holds the nozzle in his hand, he is very likely to injure himself. The high pressure of the blast injures his skin, he is cooled too rapidly, and if the blast chances to strike his eyes he may be blinded. Fan yourself with a piece of cardboard, not the air hose.)

12. Working on Humid Days

I

MUGGY DAYS LOWER HUMAN WORKING EFFICIENCY BECAUSE THE moisture in the atmosphere curtails the loss of surplus body heat. Only a little mugginess can have big effects.

When you do sedentary work in an ordinary room, for instance, about 15 per cent of your surplus body heat is removed by evaporation of insensible perspiration. As the layer of insensible perspiration on your face, neck, and hands evaporates it absorbs about 1 B.T.U. of your surplus heat. If the room air is dry enough, it can keep on evaporating that perspiration and absorbing surplus body heat at that rate, minute after minute. But if the room air is already moist, the perspiration does not evaporate so readily and your surplus heat accumulates—so you feel wilted, become inefficient, and may develop a sweaty body odor.

II

There is always water vapor—moisture—in outdoor and indoor air. We see it at times as dew, fog, mist, or frost. It is always there, even in a dry desert, whether we see it or not.

Warm air can hold more water vapor than cold air. That is the main reason why summers are muggier than winters. This is unfortunate, too, because during the summer we have more perspiration to evaporate, yet the natural conditions are less favorable for its evaporation.

The amount of water vapor in the air is spoken of as the relative humidity. It varies not only with climatic and weather conditions but also with the number of people in a room. A 30 per cent relative humidity means the air is carrying 30 per cent of the water it could if it were fully saturated. This innocent figure has a powerful influence over you.

As an illustration, let's suppose you go to work at a sedentary job in a small office crowded with workers. The room temperature is 72 degrees F., the air is becalmed, but you are comfortable and begin the day efficiently.

Each hour, however, the room air becomes more humid, because of the people in it, as they give off moisture to the air from their insensible perspiration, and lots more moisture with each breath they exhale. (All humans are close to "all wet," their bodies being more than 65 per cent water.)

A sedentary person exhales a little more than two gallons of air a minute, and this air is completely saturated with moisture as it leaves the lungs. Those who are engaged in muscle work add much more water vapor than that to the air because they exhale more air, and always saturated.

Thus by the middle of the forenoon the small office begins to get muggy because the relative humidity has risen to, say, 60 per cent, largely because of the people in the room. At that humidity the loss of surplus heat by evaporation comes almost to a standstill, and a room temperature of 72 degrees F. begins to become uncomfortable. You feel like taking a rest pause, or coffee break, but that will not give much relief unless the humidity or the temperature is lowered. If the temperature were lowered to 68 degrees F. with that relative humidity of 60 per cent, you would be comfortable again.

Suppose a fog comes up and boosts the relative humidity in that office to 90 per cent. You will then really wilt, and your efficiency will drop way down, unless somehow the room temperature can be lowered to 65 degrees F. It will likely require air conditioning to get the temperature that low, because each person in the crowded room is giving off some 400 B.T.U. of heat an hour as well as adding to the humidity.

For efficient working the relative humidity should not go above somewhere between 50 per cent and 60 per cent. It depends partly upon the cooling power of the air otherwise (temperature and air motion), and upon how much muscular activity you are doing. When strenuous muscular work is being done, the humidity needs to be lower.

III

The air over the oceans has about 85 per cent relative humidity, so countries that are blanketed by sea air are likely to be unusually

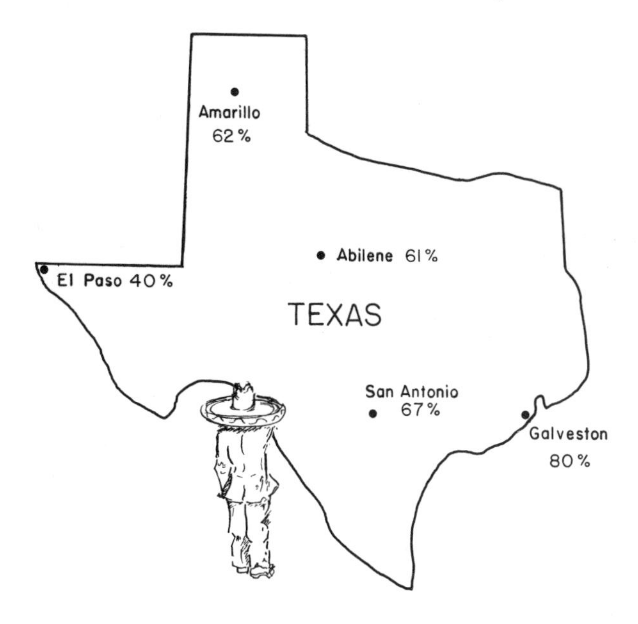

33. HOW CITIES IN ONE STATE VARY IN THEIR HUMIDITY
Average annual relative humidity

damp. Ireland, for instance, is so damp most of the year that feather pillows are flat rather than fluffy. Japan is blanketed by humid air in summer, and the people wilt despite the relatively low temperature in Tokyo. Seacoast cities and those on large lakes are also on the humid side, especially in summer. Tropical countries tend to be humid, which helps produce lush foliage but is hard on people.

The seacoasts or large river areas were settled first in most countries, because people depended upon water transportation. Some of these early settlements became today's big cities. Thus in the New

World the density of population is greatest along the coasts and larger waterways, the places with the most humid conditions. Look at the map of Texas and the list of United States cities to see what a seacoast location means for humidity.

During the winter months in the North Temperate Zone, however, the humidity is seldom oppressive outdoors. And in heated buildings the relative humidity is usually only 20 per cent to 30 per cent, except when too many people are in an unventilated room, or when moisture is added by some factory or domestic processes, as on washday. So far as is known a humidity this low has little effect on working efficiency, although there are indications that it may play a part in increasing respiratory ailments. The humidity in a heated building is difficult to raise, except at great expense, and devices in home furnaces raise the humidity barely 1 per cent or 2 per cent when they are working at their best.

The problems for personal efficiency are how to keep the humidity down during the warm and humid months and how to manage oneself so as to live with a high humidity.

RANKING OF SOME UNITED STATES CITIES ON HUMIDITY
(Average Annual Relative Humidity)

Most favorable for personal efficiency (51–60 per cent):

	Per cent		*Per cent*
Boise, Idaho	57	Rapid City, South Dakota	59
Denver, Colorado	53	Red Bluff, California	56
Fresno, California	56	Salt Lake City, Utah	52
Helena, Montana	60	Santa Fe, New Mexico	51
Lander, Wyoming	60	Winnemucca, Nevada	53

Slightly favorable for personal efficiency (61–70 per cent):

	Per cent		*Per cent*
Abilene, Texas	61	North Platte, Nebraska	68
Amarillo, Texas	62	Oklahoma City, Oklahoma	69
Dodge City, Kansas	67	Omaha, Nebraska	70
Harrisburg, Pennsylvania	70	St. Louis, Missouri	69
Havre, Montana	70	San Antonio, Texas	67
Kansas City, Missouri	69	Spokane, Washington	63
Los Angeles, California	69	Walla Walla, Washington	62
Louisville, Kentucky	68		

Least favorable for personal efficiency (71–80 per cent):

	Per cent		*Per cent*
Albany, New York	74	Montgomery, Alabama	72
Atlanta, Georgia	71	New Orleans, Louisiana	78
Atlantic City, New Jersey	79	New York, New York	71
Bismarck, North Dakota	71	Oswego, New York	76
Boston, Massachusetts	71	Palestine, Texas	73
Buffalo, New York	76	Parkersburg, West Virginia	75
Charlotte, North Carolina	71	Philadelphia, Pennsylvania	71
Chicago, Illinois	73	Port Huron, Michigan	77
Cleveland, Ohio	72	Portland, Oregon	74
Des Moines, Iowa	72	San Francisco, California	78
Duluth, Minnesota	78	St. Paul, Minnesota	72
Eastport, Maine	79	Sault Ste. Marie, Michigan	80
Galveston, Texas	80	Seattle, Washington	77
Green Bay, Wisconsin	72	Shreveport, Louisiana	72
Huron, South Dakota	72	Springfield, Illinois	72
Indianapolis, Indiana	71	Springfield, Missouri	72
Jacksonville, Florida	80	Tampa, Florida	79
Knoxville, Tennessee	73	Washington, D.C.	71
Little Rock, Arkansas	72	Wilmington, North Carolina	79
Lynchburg, Virginia	72		

IV

How can humidity be lowered to an efficient level during the summer?

We can shut the door to hot air, but humidity is not so easily shut out. Water vapor has the proclivity to migrate steadily to where the air is less saturated. The vapor will sneak in through a keyhole, through the cracks around doors and windows, down the fireplace chimney when the air indoors is drier than outdoors.

This leakage through cracks and crevices is greatly cut down in newer buildings where windows are equipped with interlocked weather stripping at the factory. These buildings may be so airtight, in fact, that there is not sufficient draft for a fireplace or furnace fire, and separate intake ducts may be needed for these (but close these ducts during humid weather when fires are not being kept).

In addition to leaking in through small openings, moisture will filter right through some walls, headed for the drier locations. Buildings of brick, stone, cement, or stucco tend to be humid inside because the walls themselves absorb rain, fog, and mist. Some bricks, for instance, will absorb a pint of water during a rain. This water vapor migrates from the damp wall into the less damp interior of the building.

Many of the old brick mansions on the New England seacoast were painted with ordinary house paint to keep rain and fog from soaking into the bricks. There are now inexpensive and colorless solutions which can be quickly sprayed on any masonry to waterproof it for about five years. But many of the colored paints used on masonry do not waterproof, and hence do little to keep the moisture out of the house; investigate the waterproofing qualities of the paint you use on masonry.

Some interior building materials have a penchant for absorbing water; unpainted wood, many kinds of wallboards, and insulating material, for instance. Again, investigate the moisture-resisting qualities of materials if you live in a humid location.

Build to be as dry as possible if you are in a humid location, and even then you will need to wring the water out of the indoor air continuously during the humid season. Air conditioners wring out some of the water. So do dehumidifiers that have automatic controls. When doing sedentary work set the control at 60 per cent relative humidity; when doing manual work set it at 50 per cent.

A personal illustration can show how indoor humidity can be controlled. At 7 A.M. one morning the relative humidity outside was 99 per cent. It was difficult to believe it was that high because indoors it was a pleasant 52 per cent. That demonstrates what air conditioning and dehumidifiers can do to create efficient working conditions.

V

The production of water vapor indoors should be kept as low as possible during the humid months. Don't scrub the floors on a humid day; you likely wouldn't feel like doing it on such a day, anyway.

The water vapor that has to be produced indoors should be promptly blown outside. A vented exhaust fan over the stove can blow much of the vapor from cooking to the outdoors through a duct. It may also lower the temperature in the kitchen. Laundry equipment can be equipped with a similar vented exhaust fan. Bathrooms, also, should have exhaust fans that are vented to the outdoors.

The vented fans in laundry and bath can be controlled by time switches on the wall which will shut a fan off when you estimate that the vapor will have been blown out.

A duct without a fan does not remove much of the vapor. The vapor has to be blown out. And a fan without a duct merely scatters the vapor around indoors; it may produce a cooling effect from air movement, but the vapor remains. For illustration, the suction of an exhaust fan in the living room or bedroom window spreads much of the vapor from kitchen and bath through the house. Have the fan close to the source of the vapor and connected with a duct to the outside where you want the moisture to go.

Bedding is likely to become musty during humid weather. Feather pillows often become limp and flat from insensible perspiration as well as moisture absorbed from the air. Sun the bedding, including the mattress. Feather pillows can be tumbled for fifteen minutes in the clothes dryer set for cool air to fluff them up again.

Summer sleep is usually more comfortable when a curled hair pillow and mattress are used. These do not absorb so much moisture as feathers and felt, and are cooler to lie on. A hair pillow is not soft, but there are nights when coolness may be more desired than softness. You will find more about temperature and sleep in our book *Sound Ways to Sound Sleep.*

Other house furnishings tend to hold moisture; rugs and carpets are prime examples. Some families who live near the seacoast roll up their rugs and store them during humid seasons. Thick upholstery also holds moisture, but this is not prevented, as some imagine, by concealing the upholstery under muslin covers. The muslin may be more comfortable than mohair to sit on during hot weather, but the mohair and padding are still there to hold moisture.

In some industrial processes it is necessary to have a high humidity. Weaving some kinds of cloth requires a humid atmosphere to prevent yarn breakages. The water sprays, steam jets, and other means that are employed to make the weaving shed humid to keep the materials in workable condition also make it a poor place for people to work. When humidity cannot be lowered because of the materials, the room can be made more efficient for workers by using fans to keep the air moving. In a humid textile mill in England, when fans were used to move the humid air at the rate of a mile-and-a-half an hour, the output increased 2.2 per cent. (Moving the air does not lower the humidity. It cools people in this situation by moving away saturated air from next to their skins so that slightly drier air can evaporate more insensible perspiration.)

Because of the proclivity of water vapor to migrate to less humid regions, the adjoining departments in a factory will become more humid when one department has to be kept humid. This can be prevented by moving the humid operation into a separate building some distance from the others, as is being done by some modern chemical plants.

VI

There are techniques to follow in dealing with perspiration. For perspiration to have its full cooling effect it has to evaporate right on the skin. What you sponge off with a handkerchief or drips off you does not cool you.

Let the perspiration accumulate and evaporate as it will. If it accumulates in such quantities that it runs off, slow down your work until the evaporation catches up with your perspiration.

"Learn to sweat like a gentleman" is advice given fledgling military officers. Let the beads stand on your brow until they evaporate. If they become so large that they trickle down your face, let them trickle, and hope they will evaporate before reaching your shoes.

The same principle applies after taking a bath on a hot day. Instead of using cold water to cool you (too rapidly), use lukewarm water. And instead of wiping yourself promptly with a towel, wriggle yourself to shake off the outer layer of water, then let most of the remainder cool you by evaporating. Don't be in a rush to wipe yourself dry—every one-half teaspoon of water that evaporates removes about 2 B.T.U. of surplus body heat. Such slow drying is safer cooling than a cold bath. If the bathroom air is especially moist, as it is likely to be, you will not evaporate much from your own wet skin unless a vented exhaust fan is used—but don't stand in front of a fan until you are dry.

VII

The water lost through perspiring needs to be replaced—remember, the body is about 65 per cent water. The more perspiration, invisible and visible, that is evaporated from your body surface, the thirstier you become. In Death Valley, California, where the summer temperature ranges from 100 degrees F. to 135 F., in the shade, the air is so dry and evaporation so rapid that when just sitting it is almost impossible to drink enough water to replace what evaporates.

Losing water by perspiring is not a successful way to lose weight, as some discover after "sweating out" in a Turkish bath. The upset water balance in the body stimulates thirst and you are impelled to drink until the balance is restored.

A football player may lose sixteen pounds from sweating during a game—nearly seven quarts of perspiration. But he is back to his pregame weight the next afternoon, thanks to the several quarts of milk he drank.

If the water balance is not restored by slow drinking of enough water, you're headed for trouble. And if you drink too much, it increases sweating and can make you, literally, waterlogged. Don't try to restore your water balance with a few big gulps, or you may have a tussle with stomach cramps. You lost the water slowly, replace it slowly—in small amounts, frequently. And don't over-replace.

Perspiration is more than water. It carries with it some of the body salts, the most important for us being sodium chloride, or ordinary table salt. It may contain as much as 0.5 per cent of salt, easily tasted in the sweat that runs down your lips. When perspiration is excessive, it carries away more salt than the body can stand to lose, and it may lead to collapse. The critical point seems to be after three quarts has been perspired. This never happens at sedentary work. A miner doing hard digging, however, may perspire a quart an hour, and he should drink not more than that nor much less.

When the perspiration is three quarts or more a day, the salt lost in it needs to be replaced. Salt tablets have been used on heavy or hot jobs to replace this loss. Scientists' observations, however, show that simply salting one's regular food a bit heavier during hot weather will make up for the salt lost on the hardest or hottest of jobs. The only advantage of salt tablets is that the person may forget to salt his food more than usual. More about this in the next chapter as we take up how to eat cool.

As a person becomes older the problems of efficient sweating become more marked. The researches by Dr. R. F. Hellon and colleagues in the Medical Research Council Unit at the University of Oxford show that people past forty do not begin to perspire as soon as they should when in a hot room. Men in their early twenties began to perspire after fifteen minutes in the heat, but men in the early fifties did not begin to perspire until they had been in the heat for twenty-nine minutes. This slowness to perspire shifts a bigger load on to the other processes by which the body gets rid of excess heat. The older men in the hot room, for instance, had a more rapid heartbeat and the internal temperature of the body was higher than in the younger men.

13. Dress Cool, Eat Cool, Think Cool

I

WHEN THE TEMPERATURE RISES TO THE MID-SEVENTIES, AND THE day is humid, your personal comfort and working efficiency will be more favorable if you dress cool, eat cool, and think cool.

Dress cool so that surplus body heat can be lost more readily.

Eat cool so that less body heat is produced.

Think cool so that you keep in a positive frame of mind and do not feel so sorry for yourself that you neglect to watch your efficiency.

To *dress cool* clothes should be chosen that will

Let the surplus body heat radiate away
Facilitate the circulation of air over your skin
Speed up the evaporation of perspiration
Protect you from nearby heat sources, including the sun.

Business and working clothes are more likely to keep the body heat in than to let it out. In one office where the room temperature was 70 degrees F. the temperature just inside the men's clothes—their *"personal climate"*—averaged 87 degrees F. And since their clothes did not facilitate the evaporation of perspiration, the relative humidity inside the envelope of dead air next to their skins was 70 per cent. Although the air in the room was favorable for efficiency, the men's skin was enclosed in a personal climate that came close to a humid tropical climate.

If clothes make the man, their clothes were making those men inefficient. (Some authorities believe, although there is not clear proof, that wearing heavy trousers with a belt that impedes air circulation inside produces a personal climate at the groin that weakens men sexually.)

The women in that office, in contrast, had a more favorable personal climate inside their clothes. The temperature for their skin was 80 degrees F., with a relative humidity of only 55 per cent—about like an average summer day at Fresno, California. The women had better cooling conditions than the men, but they were still in the unfavorable zone. The women were slightly better off because their clothing was of lighter and cooler materials (cotton, while the men wore wool). The women had added help from skirts, short sleeves, low necklines, and (some of them) no hosiery, all of which made the envelope of dead air smaller. In this aspect of the battle of the sexes the women had the advantage.

II

What should one look for when selecting warm-weather clothes? There are several qualities of clothing which everybody is familiar with but which they have not thought of as influencing their personal efficiency. As a result style and efficiency do not always go together.

First of all, materials should be of a type that do not hold body heat inside the clothes. (Wool, nylon, dacron, and some other man-made fibers are poor at letting heat through; they are more suited to cold and moderate days than to warm days. Cotton and linen fibers let heat radiate through so that the envelope of air next to the skin can cool off more.)

Loosely-woven cloth is more favorable for warm days, since it cools by allowing more air to enter through the material. The skin must "breathe." Heavily starched clothes are warm because they do not allow air to permeate to the skin. Although most clothing for workmen is made of cotton, it is woven tightly to make it wear longer, so tightly, in fact, that it is almost airtight. The only place air can get in is at the ankles, neck, and sleeves—and often not there because of cuffs or tight fit. A looser weave would not wear so well, but would do more to improve working efficiency and might be the better buy in the long run. What counts in hot weather is cooling, not wear.

Lightweight clothing is usually cooler, but not always. Nylon and dacron cloth are thin and lightweight, but are hot inside because those fibers hold heat, and the fabric is so tightly woven that air cannot penetrate. Don't judge solely on the basis of lightness—a plastic bag is light. Hold the material to the light to see if there are the desirable open spaces to ventilate that envelope of dead air. Better yet, try blowing smoke through it; blow gently, because when the garment is worn there will be only gentle air currents to ventilate your personal climate.

Ventilated shoes and strap sandals allow more air circulation to the feet. If you don't wear them on hot days, kick the others off under the desk.

You will be more comfortable heat-wise if you wear loosely fitting clothes that are tailored with ample slack. Cheap ones often skimp on material and are not so loose as they should be. Really loose clothing—such as Edison insisted upon—allows for more air to circulate next to the skin. In addition, loose garments create air movement inside as they flap when you walk or move. Skirts, including the kilts of Scotland, have a marked fanning effect when the wearer moves. The hoop skirt was as effective as an oriental punkah in producing a personal breeze, but much of this breeze was wasted owing to the ankle-length pantalettes that were worn (most of the time) under the skirts. The desert Arabs, who have learned to live with intense heat, wear long, flowing robes that fan next to their skin as they move.

Tight regions in clothing are bottlenecks that prevent the movement of cooling air. Belts, collars, cuffs, and girdles are the principal offenders. Loosen them, or do away with them if possible during warm spells.

The more bare skin that is exposed to the room air, the cooler. Every extra square inch of bare skin helps—except in the sun. Short skirts, short sleeves, shorts, open collars, if you can get by with them at work. If you wear long sleeves, roll them up, but loosely. Some city police and state troopers are permitted to wear short-sleeved, open-neck shirts, no coats, during hot weather. Hosiery, though sheer, is made of fibers that hold in the heat; there is less strain on the body's cooling system if hosiery is rolled down, or dispensed with, during hot weather.

III

What if one has to work in the sun?

The lighter-colored your outer garments the better, whether you work in the sun or merely walk in it—of course you are not foolish enough to lie in it. White clothes are best because they reflect 80 per cent of the solar energy and allow only 20 per cent of the sun's heat to penetrate the garment. Black reflects only 12 per cent of the solar heat and passes 88 per cent of it on to your personal climate.

Color has little effect when indoors but does make a real difference when you are in the sun. Don't dress like a funeral director in the summer. White or very light colors for summer, dark colors if you want them for winter.

The Arabs who live in blistering desert heat wear white almost religiously.

The widely worn blue denim work clothes are unfavorable in color as well as tightness of weave. The color was adopted largely because it did not show dirt, not for promoting personal efficiency. The white overalls used by masons and painters are much more favorable for outdoor summer work.

Protect yourself from the sun.

The Arabs protect themselves from the burning desert sun by headdresses and flowing robes of loosely woven material that cover all the body except hands and face. Deaths from sunstroke would be common if they did not take those precautions. Protection from their extreme sun conditions is a life-and-death matter for them. It may sometimes be a life-and-death matter in the North Temperate Zone, too. In the United States, for instance, there are 520 deaths from sunstroke or heat prostration in an average year; there were 1,401 in the hot year of 1952; four times as many men as women. Be temperate in exposing yourself to direct sunlight.

Wear a head covering whenever you are outside and the temperature is above 80 degrees F. Light-colored, of course. A wide-brimmed straw hat is excellent, as the Mexicans and the Chinese discovered long ago. Have the brim wide enough to shade shoulders as well as face, neck, and bald spot. If the crown is not ventilated, poke a few holes in the sides of the crown—not in the top where the sun's rays could come through to your head.

Construction workers often fashion a head covering from a small bath towel, after the manner of the Arabs, so that the ends drape over their shoulders. These do not obstruct vision at work or "get in the way" as a straw cartwheel would. Such head coverings can be given additional cooling power by soaking them in water, which will lower the temperature of the covering as the water evaporates. But this wetting helps only in dry climates; unless the water evaporates speedily it will only add to the heat burden of your body by slowing the evaporation of insensible perspiration.

Clothing that becomes soaked with sweat also adds to the burden of your cooling system, except in very dry climates. The fact that clothes stay wet indicates that the climate is not dry enough to evaporate rapidly. So change to dry clothes, rinse the wet garments, and hang them in the sun to dry.

During harvest periods some farm workers hang their wet clothes on fences and put on dry outfits about every hour. They are the workers who do not get heat prostration.

Foundry and blast furnace workers are usually urged to switch to dry clothes when they rest between the pourings of heats of molten metal. Some foundries have rope halyards, similar to flagpole ropes, by which workers can hoist their rinsed set of clothes up close to the chimney where the heat will dry them rapidly. A variation of the wash-and-wear system.

IV

What kind of clothes are protective clothes?

There is a considerable variety, and their usual purpose is to protect the worker from injury or accident. Shoes with steel toes, for instance, to protect the toes from falling objects. Tough helmets to protect the head. Goggles to protect the eyes. Rubber gloves to protect from chemicals or electrical shock. Gloves of steel mesh to protect fingers when using a knife.

Our interest in this chapter is in protective clothing which may interfere with getting rid of surplus body heat. For example, there are chemical processes where workers have to be covered from head to toe in rubberized garments to protect them from chemicals. This kind of protective clothing is likely to be both airtight and moisture-tight—much like being inside a plastic bag. It can safely be worn only a few minutes at a time.

The way the heart rate goes skyward when such impenetrable clothing is worn gives an idea of how great the bodily stress is when surplus heat cannot be lost. Dr. Lucien A. Brouha reported pulse rates averaging 180 beats per minute after a half-hour of work wearing an impervious suit. When exactly the same work was done while wearing a suit which "let the skin breathe," the pulse averaged 142 beats per minute.

When workers have to work in front of heat sources, as in smelters and blast furnaces, protective clothing of asbestos cloth is sometimes used to deflect the intense heat from their bodies. The weave of the cloth allows some air to penetrate and the skin can breathe a little. Faces may be shielded from the direct heat by helmets resembling those worn by welders.

The most effective heat-protecting suit has been developed in Du Pont's Haskell Laboratory by Dr. Brouha. Coveralls and a ventilated hood were tailored from a cloth that allowed the skin to breathe. Then an air hose was installed inside the coveralls to provide additional inside ventilation by forcing currents of air between the skin and the garment.

This suit with the built-in forced ventilation was tested on men who were removing sludge from the bottom of a vat of molten magnesium. Very hot work. The men used an iron ladle with a ten-foot-long handle to keep them as far away as possible from the heat source. A face shield protected their faces from the heat, and a respirator over nose and mouth protected them from the chlorine fumes that came from the vat.

When the men did that work wearing their usual work clothes plus the face mask and respirator, their pulse rates averaged 127 beats per minute after ten minutes' work.

Then the same desludging was done while wearing the new suit and hood with the forced ventilation built in. They did not need the face shield and respirator because the forced ventilation inside the hood kept the chlorine fumes away from them. After a ten-minute

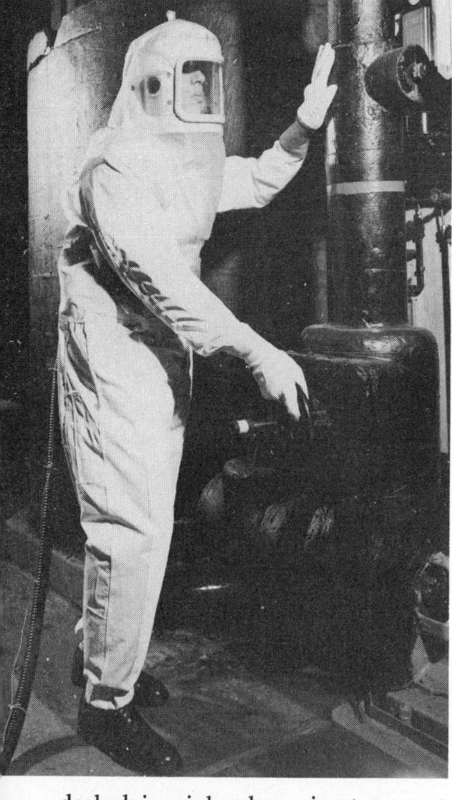

34. An air-conditioned protective suit for hot work places. Description in text. (Courtesy E. I. duPont de Nemours & Company)

desludging job when air at room temperature (90 per cent F.) had been forced through the suit, the pulse rates averaged 111 per minute. Better working conditions than when the suit was not worn.

For the next test the suit and hood were ventilated with cool air. After ten minutes of desludging with that envelope of cool air the pulse rates were only 92 a minute. Vastly better conditions. There was no stress worth speaking of on their bodies, and their working efficiency was greatly increased.

How much their efficiency was increased is illustrated by one worker. When he wore his usual clothes, plus the face mask and respirator, he could ladle out 134 pounds of sludge in ten minutes. With the air-cooled suit and hood he ladled out 320 pounds during the same time.

Clothes do make the man in more ways than are usually dreamed of. To be a better man—or woman—during warm weather wear clothes that let your surplus body heat out, whether you work in a smelter or in an office, and thus bring the personal climate inside your clothes to a more favorable zone.

V

To *eat cool* for better efficiency in warm weather we should

Eat sparingly of foods that increase body heat production
Drink and eat to make up for the loss of water and salt
Shrink the layer of fat which slows down the loss of surplus heat.

Toward the end of a hearty meal or banquet people often comment about the room being too hot. Beads of perspiration may collect on their foreheads. Puzzlingly, however, the room thermometer is no higher than usual. What makes them feel so warm?

They feel warm because the specific dynamic action (S.D.A.) of foods raises their body temperatures slightly. This unexpected effect was first suspected by Dr. Max Rubner, a pioneer in the scientific study of foods who later directed one of the first laboratories to study the physiology of work. In 1885 he had observed that body-heat production was increased after eating a large meal. He continued to experiment on this, and in 1902 published a book, in German, which showed how foods do have a dynamic effect on the activity of body cells.

As a result of this dynamic effect, bodily metabolism and heat production are raised for the time being. This heat is not owing to work, but to a chemical stimulation by ingredients in the foods. Although the heat is not because of work, we still have the warm-weather problem of getting rid of it—and of cutting it down in the first place.

It is because of the S.D.A. that your physician makes sure you have not eaten for twelve hours when he gives you a basal metabolism test.

This dynamic action, or waste-heat production, is apparent about a half-hour after we start to eat, and reaches its peak about three hours after eating, then tapers off for a couple more hours. Altogether, about five hours of increased heat production after eating a square meal. The bigger the meal, the greater the S.D.A.

All foods have some S.D.A., but it is much greater for some. Fats have least S.D.A., increasing heat production only about 4 per cent. Carbohydrates have a little more, stimulating a 6 per cent increase in heat. Proteins are way ahead of the others, increasing the body's heat production by about 30 per cent!

There is no doubt that proteins should be eaten sparingly when we wish to avoid that big increase in (waste) heat production. Foods that are high in protein, and which should be eaten only in small servings and only occasionally in warm weather, are:

Meats
Cheese
Fish
Beans
Fowl
Eggs

Yet those are almost staples for the assorted cold cuts that people favor during hot weather! The coldness of the food misleads the unwary. Although the protein may be eaten cold, its S.D.A. still boosts heat production by nearly one third.

Summer is the time to emphasize salads, vegetables, and fruits. The protein foods are better for winter than summer.

Vegetarians have a low-protein diet. Strict vegetarians have a basal metabolism some 10 per cent lower than meat eaters. It is fortunate for the people of hot India that their religion forces the majority to be vegetarians the year around. It is unfortunate for the desert Arabs that they cannot grow many vegetables and so have to live in that scorching climate on a high-meat diet.

More liquids are needed during hot weather to replace the water that is lost from the body by perspiring. Thirst is not a satisfactory guide, because we usually do not pause to drink until we become very thirsty. Most people need to drink a little more water than they do during hot weather, but they should not go to the extreme of drinking all they can swallow. Drink a small amount as soon as you feel only slightly thirsty, don't wait until you are parched and then gulp a large amount. If you want to keep track of how much you drink, use paper cups instead of the bubbler; in some hot jobs industrial physicians prescribe the number of cups per day.

Coffee or tea—either hot or cold—may be used to replace the water loss. But if either is used in large amounts, both increase the basal heat production. This is not an S.D.A. effect but is because of the caffeine in coffee, or theobromine in tea, which "pep up" a person so that he becomes more active and produces body heat by moving around a little more. Cola-type carbonated beverages contain caffeine and sugar about equal to a cup of highly sweetened coffee.

Alcoholic beverages are not effective for replacing the water loss. They stimulate the production of urine so that water may be lost rather than replaced. In addition, the alcohol, which is absorbed from the stomach itself, makes the skin warmer. Alcoholic drinks are more suited to winter than summer months.

Since perspiration carries away sodium chloride (table salt) as well as water, we need to increase the use of salt during warm weather. For office work and other sedentary occupations this salt loss can be made up merely by salting the food a little more than usual. The person doing a little heavier work, and perspiring more, should use a little more salt. It is not necessary to take salt tablets. During hot weather take your food as you do politicians' promises—with a few extra grains of salt.

There are also indications that when a person perspires profusely for several days he should increase his vitamin C intake. Citrus fruits, tomatoes, strawberries, and most other fruits are good sources. Drink more orange, grapefruit, and tomato juice during hot weather and replace the water loss at the same time you are increasing the vitamin C intake.

But bear in mind that these juices are also foods, and you should cut down your meals slightly if you drink those juices between meals. A can of beer has some 110 calories, a cup of orange juice 100, a cup of tomato juice 50, black unsweetened coffee or plain water, zero calories. A cup of milk contains 160 calories, and a bottle of soda pop 110 calories. And calories are important in hot weather, as we shall now discover.

A sure way to slow down the loss of surplus body heat and be uncomfortable in warm weather is to be fat. A little fat will do it, you don't have to be fat enough for the sideshow. A thin layer of fat slows down the heat loss greatly—about like wearing a suit of woollen underwear underneath your skin.

If you must be overweight, limit it to the winter months; the fat will be a real comfort in keeping you warm. But if you want it to feel like "the good old summertime," be on the thin side before the mercury starts to climb.

You will have to outwit your appetite during the summer if you want to stay on the lean side. You are likely to want to eat more during hot weather and will have to use self-control to stop eating when you should. The United States Army Medical Research and Nutrition Laboratory tested men who worked and ate in a hot temperature of 105 degrees F. for ten days, then for another ten days when the temperature was 78 degrees F. The men could follow their appetites and eat all they wanted, any time. During the hot period the average man ate 400 calories more each day, and gained weight!

Stand, undressed, in front of a mirror, and take a deep breath. Can you see the outlines of most of your ribs as you hold that deep breath? If you can't, you have on a suit of fatty underwear that makes you uncomfortable and less efficient in hot weather. Ask your family physician how to take off that fat. Or perhaps your employer has trained dieticians, as the Eastman Kodak Company has, who will help you work out a balanced diet to get your weight down to where it will help comfort, efficiency, and well-being.

VI

Think cool. Figuratively speaking, of course.

Think positively about what you can do to lower the room temperature, to get some air circulation, to lose your surplus body heat, to dress and eat more as you should. Not negatively about how uncomfortable it is, or how unlucky you are because you can't be loafing in the cool Maine woods.

Turn your thoughts to what you are working at. Think about your work, not your perspiration.

Give yourself a mental set to keep on the alert for accuracy and safety in your work—errors and accidents tend to increase on hot days.

And don't expect to accomplish as much as you would if the temperature were 70 degrees F., the relative humidity 50 per cent, and the air gently moving. But keep on working, anyway.

14. What You Should Know About Noise

I

Do the noises that bombard moderns affect their working efficiency?

It is easy to be annoyed by a noise, especially when it comes at an unexpected moment and interrupts our work. Mark Twain's home in Hartford was one of the first in the world to have a telephone, and the famous humorist was proud as punch about it at first. Shortly, however, he took an intense dislike to what he considered its noisy ringing. On one occasion he became so infuriated that he called the operator to "send down and take this damned thing out of here." And one Christmas he wrote that he wanted everybody to go to heaven except the inventor of the telephone.

A few people—perhaps one out of a hundred—think noises are frightful nuisances and terribly irritating. Noises "set their nerves on edge" and bring out extreme behavior. A nationally known physician in Kansas City, for example, was so upset when an air hammer began pounding away in front of his home that he rushed out in a frenzy and fought the workmen. (He lost the fight, even though he was six feet two inches and a redhead.)

Such people have a neurotic dread of noise. They write letters to newspapers complaining about local noises, and call law officers to quiet barking dogs. Or they start campaigns to have garbage cans made of rubber. One city health commissioner said that so many "cranks on noise" pestered him with their complaints that he scarcely had time to take care of important health problems.

These people also fuss about noise in the office or home. Some can't stand the squeak of a door hinge. The grinding sound of the pencil sharpener upsets them so they can't work for fifteen minutes. A slamming drawer makes them jump almost out of their skins. If the window shade flaps in the breeze, they put on a scene that halts production for a few minutes.

Are such people overly sensitive to noises because they have especially sharp ears? No; and neither do the noises hurt their ears. They are usually "the nervous sort" who react excessively—and emotionally, as that physician did—to sounds that other people hear just as sharply but without going to extremes. Some people of this sort may not mind noises, but, instead, complain about drafts, or get annoyed because their food is not seasoned to suit them, or react with violent disgust at gum chewers. They just have to have something to be particular and annoyed about. Elimination of noises would not lessen their "edginess," but psychotherapy might.

Since this embattled minority complains forcefully about what they presume noise is doing to them, they have given bystanders a misleading impression about inherent dangers in the noises in our world. They also lower their own efficiency by wasting time fussing about noises and by their upset emotional attitudes when they hear a noise. In our world there will always be noises to upset them.

II

Most people, in contrast, plod along stolidly without wondering whether noise affects their efficiency or not. A person who works in a noisy place usually says the noise bothered him a bit at first, but that he soon got used to it and now feels it doesn't affect his work.

How wrong this average person's impression can be, however, is shown by Dr. Mack T. Henderson's tests of the effects of radio music on studying. This "pleasant noise" lowered study efficiency, even for those who said they liked to study with the radio on and who believed that it helped rather than interfered with their study.

→ Although noise is not the dire evil that the embattled minority imagines, it does have more influence on human efficiency than the majority realizes. Most of us need to do something to control some of the noises in our environment if we are to make fuller use of our abilities.

III

Just what does noise do to people?

The evidence has been summed up by D. E. Broadbent, of the Medical Research Council Applied Psychology Unit, in a report to The Royal Society for the Promotion of Health. The statements in this section are a summary of his summary.

There is no clear proof that noises have any lingering effects on mental health when we are away from the noise. We may have a ringing in the ears after being around an intense noise, but only for a short time. People who work day after day in intense noise, however, may become slightly deafened; this sometimes occurs to boilermakers and men who operate air hammers to break up pavements. It is an open question whether continued exposure to such intense noises produces any other lingering effects on health.

When talking is required in the work, efficiency is almost always lowered by noise. As the "Noise Thermometer" shows, the average office or noisy home is slightly louder than average conversations. When the noise in the environment is louder than the conversation, we have to listen more closely, or shout, or both. Instructions and details are more likely to be missed, or misunderstood, in a noisy place. We become hoarse from trying to talk above the noise of a subway or some busy restaurants or company cafeterias.

If you have to raise your voice, or strain in order to hear, the place is too noisy for work that requires any talking. Workers in some noisy occupations—riveters, for example—use a system of hand signals to communicate with one another about work details. Some factories try to hire deaf people for work with machines which would be deafening to normal ears.

Noise also has an adverse effect when people are doing some prolonged task which requires sustained attention and in which the same processes have to be done over and over again. Close watching of a radar screen or other instruments, or continuous mental arithmetic, or serious study are tested examples. Presumably the efficiency on jobs that require sustained attention would be lowered most.

The suspected reason why such work is especially vulnerable to noise is reflected in the old adage that you can't give attention to two things at the same time. The noise, especially if it is intermittent, or

35. NOISE THERMOMETER
(Numerals show decibles of loudness)

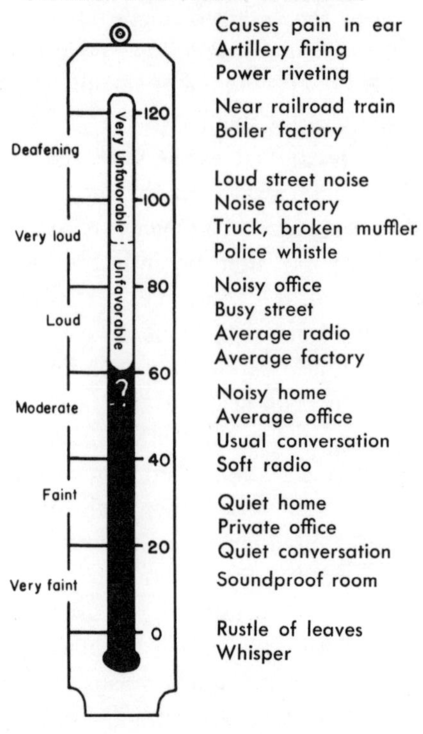

comes at unexpected times, draws attention from the work, so affects accuracy as well as output, and makes conditions favorable for accidents. The way most people in an office look up from their work when someone sneezes is an illustration, unless the office is so noisy that the sneeze is not heard.

IV

That suspicion was confirmed by comparisons of how noise affected some people more than others who were doing the same work. Extroverted people were most influenced; introverted people were affected least, and some of them apparently not at all by ordinary amounts of noise.

It is the nature of extroverted people to give attention to what is going on around them; they are more distractible, likely to work by fits and starts, jumping from one thing to another. They tend to direct their attention away from themselves, so make good salespeople and receptionists.

Introverted people, in contrast, are less interested in what is going on around them, and turn their attention inward to their own thoughts, or to what they are doing. They can concentrate for longer times on their work. Introverted people make good bookkeepers, auditors, and students. Radio music while studying should have less effect on the introverted student than on the extroverted.

It is interesting to note that the extroverted person, who is the easier distracted by noise, is also the one who is more likely to make more noise. The extroverted tends to be more active, to move around more, and to be less painstaking—all of which can produce needless noise to distract other extroverted people.

V

What kinds of noises are most likely to lower personal efficiency? And how can we reduce, or eliminate, or move them away?

A little noise may actually help efficiency, perhaps because it keeps us from becoming lonesome. This would occur mostly for noises that are no louder than those in the faint noise zone on the thermometer.

At the other extreme, noises of 90 decibels or louder are almost always seriously detrimental. Reduce them, or isolate them and let a deaf person work there.

In between those extremes efficiency begins to be lowered after the noise reaches a loudness of about 60 decibels. If the work requires talking, it is affected by less loudness. As the loudness increases, other continuous work is likely to be interfered with.

The kind of a noise, as well as how loud it is, is also a factor.

High-pitched noises are worse than those of medium pitch. The squeal of a poorly tuned radio, the squeak of a hinge, screech of skidding tires, or a cat's meowing are annoying out of proportion to their loudness because they are high pitched.

Intermittent, irregular, periodic, or warbling noises are also detrimental out of proportion to their loudness. They have more power to draw attention away from work than a steady whir or hum would. Thus the occasional hammering of a steam radiator is worse than the steady grinding of a lathe.

36. The noise the other person makes is the most distracting. (From booklet "Growing Pains;" courtesy the Connecticut Mutual Life Insurance Company)

VI

The noise someone else makes is likely to be more annoying, or distracting, than the noise we make ourselves. When a clerk uses a calculating machine on her desk for a few minutes, it is the people at the adjoining desks who get the fidgets. Father can read the evening paper easily enough when he has turned on the radio beside him, but can't stand the noise coming from the radio Jimmy has on in the adjoining room. "I don't see why it bothered him, it didn't bother me," the other fellow says.

Related to this is the tendency for noises that are irrelevant to the work at hand to be harder on our efficiency. We expect certain noises from the equipment we are using, or from what we will do next, so they do not catch us unaware and distract our attention. The unexpected noises—something dropped, a slammed door—catch us by surprise and forcefully draw attention from what we are doing.

Perhaps that is why we are likely to blame the other person, or the company, or the city, for noises that pester us and overlook the fact that we ourselves are the other person to the other person. It is good policy not only to try to reduce the noises that need reducing in our own surroundings, but also to produce fewer of them to disturb other people's surroundings or catch them by surprise and draw their minds from their work.

15. What You Can Do About Noise

I

HOW CAN WE CONTROL OR REDUCE NOISE?

Noises are tricky; they do unexpected things. They can come in through a keyhole when everything else is closed against them. They may be telegraphed through the floors to the rest of a building from a noisy machine in a far-off corner. If there are two machines reverberating loudly in a room, the noise will not be cut in half by stopping one machine. A thick stone wall will keep noises from coming in from outside but will make the noises originating inside the room louder than ever.

Such tricks need a qualified acoustical engineer's know-how when a factory or office is to be noise conditioned. But the individual worker or homeowner can do much to make noises less of an interference with his work or leisure if he follows these rules:

Muffle the noise at its source
Isolate it
Absorb it
Mask it
Don't listen to it.

II

Muffle the noise at its source by working on linoleum instead of metal or glass table and desk tops, for instance. Adjust telephone bells so that they ring more softly, or use a chime instead of a bell. Door checks prevent the noise of slamming doors. Resilient floors are quieter to walk on than hard ones. Plastic wastebaskets are quieter than metal. Consider such noise factors when buying equipment.

When buying machines, also consider the noise they make when running. A cheap electric fan or food mixer is usually much noisier than a higher-priced one.

Proper maintenance can also lessen some noises at their sources. Door hinges and swivel chairs can be oiled to eliminate their squeaks; this is done routinely every six months in some offices. Keep windows tight to prevent rattles. Keep bearings on machines tightened. When a machine becomes noisy from wear, have it overhauled, or trade it in.

People themselves are one of the chief sources of needless and bothersome noise. Muffle yourself once in a while. Figure how to do it more quietly before you make a noise if someone is within disturbing distance. Be the "quiet sort," and see the difference it makes. For instance:

Talk no louder than necessary; don't shout, shriek, yell.
Close drawers and doors gently; don't slam-bang them shut.
Keep your radio tuned low; don't make it a public distractor.
Lay things down softly; don't drop them or wham them down.
Walk quietly; don't sound like a horse in the house.
Lift chairs when you move them; don't scrape them across the floor.
Laugh quietly to yourself; don't haw-haw like a mule in the office.

When you have to hammer or make some unavoidable disturbing noise, warn the people around you before you start pounding. It will disturb them less if it does not surprise them, and if they realize it is necessary, or relevant.

When everyone tries to do things the quieter way, most offices and homes will be much less distracting than they are today.

III

When noise is inevitable, *isolate* it by

Shutting it out
Moving it away
Moving away from it

Preventing its transmission by drum-head action
Keeping it from being telegraphed to other locations.

Shut noise out by closing windows against traffic noises. Plate glass shuts out more than ordinary glass. A double-glazed window shuts out more than a single-glazed window. Joseph Pulitzer, the newspaper tycoon who was neurotically sensitive to noise, had triple-glazed plate-glass windows on his sleeping room. Weather stripping also helps. A

37. The most annoying noises are those made by other people and which are not necessary noises. Adults can be as thoughtlessly noisy as children. (From the booklet "Needlepoints;" courtesy the Connecticut Mutual Life Insurance Company)

row of tall evergreen trees shuts out some of the highway noise, but the trees must be tall and their branches touching.

Shut out noise by closing doors. Shut the kitchen door so the rattle of pots and pans will be less disturbing in other parts of the house; if your kitchen does not have a door, too bad. Light weight and hollow-core doors are less effective. There are patented doors that are most effective to keep noise from speading from music practice rooms, engine test chambers, and other noisy rooms; effective, but expensive, though worth it in some situations. Weather stripping helps, even if it is an inside door.

38. Special ear muffs are used to protect the ears when working in locations that are extremely noisy. (Courtesy Bausch & Lomb Inc.)

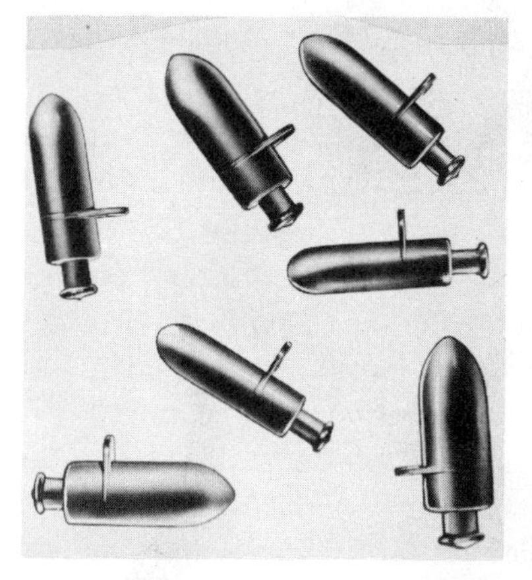

39. Noise reducing ear stopples are inserted into the ear canal to increase efficiency and prevent deafness when working in noisy locations. Made of soft flexible rubber to fit the curves and irregularities of the canal, the stopples also come in various sizes to fit different ears. Some people need a larger stopple in one ear than the other. Homemade plugs of dry cotton do not reduce the noise heard. (Courtesy Surgical Mechanical Research, Inc.)

Shut noise out of your ears by using ear stopples or special noise-reducing ear muffs. Drugstores sell special rubber or wax plugs for cutting down noises. The rubber plugs used by swimmers are also effective. A wad of dry cotton stuffed in the ears does not cut down the tricky noise. A University of Minnesota scientist, who has five small children, wears rubber ear plugs when working evenings at home.

In one textile mill the girls working in the weaving department said they were used to the loud whirring of the machines and the noise did not affect them. Industrial psychologists persuaded the girls to experiment with ear plugs, wearing the plugs one week but not the next. There was a very slight increase in output during the weeks the girls used the plugs, but not enough to insist that the plugs be continued. However, the girls wanted to keep using the plugs since they felt less worn out at the end of the day.

Move the noise source away by putting noisy work in a separate room, and keep its door closed. In one editorial office a special room is used where printers' proofs are read aloud, so that the voices are not heard in the "bullpen." If the noise source cannot be moved to another room, then put it in a far corner and hem it in with filing cabinets, packing cases, or, better, by screens of sound-absorbing material.

One housewife whose home had an open-area floor plan with no kitchen door moved the food mixer into the small utility room. The garbage grinder couldn't be moved, so she uses that only when her husband is out of the house.

Move away from the noise by getting farther away from the source. A house set far back from the street gets a little less traffic din. The upper floors in a skyscraper get much less traffic noise.

A room at the back of the house usually gets less traffic noise than a front room. Some families move to the suburbs to get away from city noise—and some are unlucky enough to have a super highway built beside their dream house a few years later.

Moving away from the noise helped a group of workers who were assembling delicate temperature regulators. Their own work was quiet, but they had been working next to a very noisy operation. After they were moved to a quieter location their output went up 26

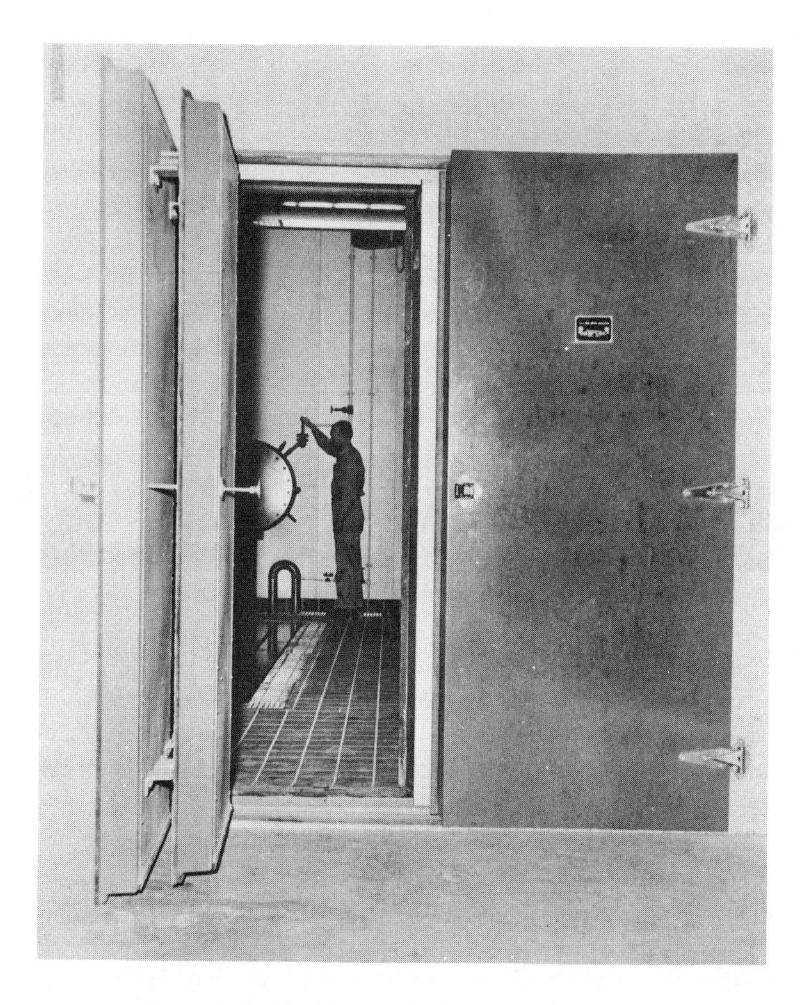

40. DOORS THAT SHUT NOISE OUT

When these acoustic doors are closed the noise is reduced by more than 60 decibels. A pneumatic riveter inside the room would sound about as loud as average conversation outside the room, or average factory noise would faintly pass through the doors. This type of door is used when noisy operations are isolated so they will not lower the efficiency of other work. The construction of the doors gives an idea of the difficulty of reducing noises. Each door is in effect two doors four inches thick and filled with sound-deadening material; the doors are separated by an air space. When closed they fit snugly into acoustical seals which are built into the matching door frame. (Courtesy Industrial Acoustics Company, Inc.)

per cent. When in the noisy location there had been imperfections in 75 per cent of their assemblies; in the quieter location only 7 per cent had imperfections.

Prevent drum-head transmission of noise by locating noisy operations away from inside partitions. Partitions often transmit the noise to the adjoining room. A sewing machine or typewriter will be less likely to disturb people in the next room if it is placed against an outside wall.

Noise is transmitted readily through partitions made of dry wallboard on 2 x 2 studs, as in many prefabricated houses; these homes have little privacy from one room to the next. A partition of lath and plaster on 2 x 4 studs is better, but loud conversation and other noises can go through. Transmission from one room to the next is still less when a second partition is built an inch or two away from the original one; some companies erect such double partitions in rooms where especially noisy machines are used.

Solid masonry partitions are least likely to transmit noises to adjoining rooms, but they are expensive and heavier than some foundations can support.

Prevent noise from being telegraphed to other locations by cutting the telegraph lines. A sponge-rubber pad under the typewriter or food mixer cuts down the noise vibrations that are otherwise telegraphed (plus some drum-head action) through the desk or bench itself. Replace the pad before it loses its resiliency.

There are several patented mountings that can be used underneath printing presses and other heavy machinery so that their rumble or thump is not telegraphed throughout the building.

When buildings are erected on bedrock, as in New York City, it sometimes happens that the noise from a heavy machine in Company A's building is telegraphed through foundations and bedrock to disturb Company B's offices.

Pipes inside a building often telegraph noise. Cut this down by keeping the pipes from touching the walls; an inch clearance which can be packed with fiber glass all around the pipe. Telegraphing through the pipes can be prevented by installing patented flexible sections that dampen the vibrations.

Telegraphing noise by hot-air or air-conditioning ducts can be lessened by using a special fabric boot to replace a section of the duct near the heater or blower.

IV

Absorb the noise to lower its loudness. The noise in a room is prolonged and made worse because the sound is bounced back and forth from hard wall surfaces.

Wood, concrete, plaster, glass, and metal reflect 97 per cent or more of the sound energy that strikes them. A room is practically an echo chamber unless the furnishings are highly sound absorbent. A common example is a bare hallway, which makes a first-class speaking tube unless a thick carpet or a ceiling of sound-absorbing material is installed.

Thick-pile fabrics will absorb up to 50 per cent of the sound that strikes them. Furniture upholstered in mohair will absorb much more than leather or plastic upholstery, and considerably more than tapestry upholstery. Thick rugs will absorb more than thin ones do. Velour drapes will absorb more than chintz. The more porous a material is, the more it will quiet a room, and the thicker the porous material the more it will quiet, especially the bass noises.

In addition to fabrics, there are special building materials that absorb noise and which can be used in place of plaster. Some lose their noise-absorbing power, however, if they are painted so that the pores become sealed. Others have drilled holes that are too large for paint to fill. These materials absorb from 12 per cent to 80 per cent of the sound hitting them, depending largely upon the thickness and kind of material.

Generous use of absorbing materials and furnishings will do much to make any place distinctly quieter, unless a punch press is whamming away at your elbow. In our own home, for illustration, the ceilings of all rooms except the baths and laundry (where the material might hold moisture) are of paintable drilled acoustical tiles that absorb about 20 per cent of the noise that strikes them, floors are covered with thick rugs under which there are equally thick felt pads, furniture is tapestry and mohair upholstered.

That absorption of sound has one drawback for us—it soaks up so much noise that we cannot talk from one room to the other, even with doors open. We either have to walk to the other room, or use the intercom—or, frequently, simply decide that what we were going to say didn't need saying, after all, which also probably helps the personal efficiency of all concerned.

Absorbing materials on ceilings and furniture, however, will not stop noises from being telegraphed through the floors and plumbing, or being air-borne in the heating ducts, or transmitted by drum-head action of flimsy partitions.

V

Mask the more irritating noises—intermittent, high-pitched, etc.—with a less annoying noise. Don't try to drown out the undesirable noise, just add one that is more agreeable to hear, or which will make the explosive peaks less noticeable. "Acoustical perfume," it has been called.

Background music, softly played, is sometimes used to mask the irregular ringing of telephone bells and other noises around an office. The handyman in his basement shop disturbs the rest of the house less if he runs his drill press idly so its hum will mask the squealing noise he makes while filing metal.

Singing while you work is sometimes an application of masking. "I sing when using the vacuum cleaner," Gladys said, "because then I don't hear the cleaner so much."

When a fight breaks out in a night club, the orchestra masks it by playing full blast.

VI

When firemen broke into a burning house in New Jersey they discovered a husband and wife calmly playing checkers. The checker players had not heard the noise of the fire sirens or of the firemen breaking into the house. Deaf? Too much sound absorption in their house? No—they were just so absorbed in their game that they were *not listening to noise*.

It is fortunate that people can become so absorbed that they do not hear noises, because this is a noisy world and is likely to continue to be so. It may get noisier as cities grow, traffic multiplies, offices become larger, and jet planes fill the sky.

A suggestion about how not to listen to noise came from one of the first experiments on the effects of noise, made by Drs. E. E. Cassel and K. M. Dallenbach, at Cornell University. In addition to finding that intermittent noises were more distracting, they discovered that some people were distracted more than others.

The people who had a passive attitude toward the noise, who accepted it as "just one of those things" to put up with, tended to ignore the noise, and consequently their work was not affected as much. You will recall that extroverted people—who are more inclined to work by fits and starts and to switch their attention to things around them—were more affected by noise.

Muffle, isolate, absorb, and mask all the noise you can. Then don't listen to the remainder. You might as well be stoical about it, and put up, unflinchingly, with what noise is unavoidable. No use running out to fight the man with the air hammer. Screw up your attention to your work instead.

Make it a habit to buckle down to work to get your mind off the noise that cannot be eliminated. And also make it a habit to do your own work more quietly; maybe the noisy fellow will imitate you.

16. The Will-To-Work Despite Hindrances

I

WE WOULD GET MUCH MORE DONE, AND DONE BETTER, IF WE ONLY kept our thoughts on our work more of the time. Distractions, discomforts, and disinterest are forever pulling our thoughts away.

There is a sudden noise, for instance, which distracts thoughts from what our hands are doing, so we make an error, or possibly have an accident. Or someone talks to us and distracts our thoughts so we lose the thread of what we were reading. Or the room may be too hot, or humid, so it is difficult to make our thoughts stay put on our work. Hunger—as when no breakfast was eaten—or tired feelings late in the day also tend to make it difficult to keep thoughts on what we are doing.

But we are also often inefficient because of self-distractions. The environmental conditions may be ideal for work, but we neglect to keep our minds on the work. We let our thoughts roam, instead of concentrating on the job.

A school library, for instance, is about as free from distractions as any place. Yet when Dr. D. C. Troth kept tabs on the amount of time the students obviously let their minds wander from their work, he found that about 40 per cent of their library study time was spent on self-distractions. The students drew doodles, looked out the window, played with their fingernails, watched a girl, fell half-asleep, counted their money. Almost as much time was spent in such non-productive activities as in studying. What made them so scatter-brained that they lost twenty-four minutes out of every hour in the library?

People who get things done, in contrast, keep their minds on their work even when the environmental conditions might be powerfully distracting. Sir Arthur Conan Doyle, the physician who turned author and wrote the famous Sherlock Holmes detective stories, is a good example. He could work in the midst of tumultuous hindrances. His small daughter would play with the bear's skull he kept on his desk, yet he would not slow down his writing. Newspaper photographers would scramble around his desk, taking Sir Arthur's picture, but apparently he did not notice them as he wrote as usual. Friends would gather in the little blue-papered room and visit unrestrainedly with each other, yet Sir Arthur would ignore them and keep right on writing. Impolite, perhaps, but highly efficient concentration.

Could those flighty students have been taught to work despite hindrances, as Sir Arthur did? Quite possibly. There are several techniques that help one concentrate, although Sir Arthur did not need them. The most important aid for working despite hindrances is the will-to-work, of which he had a large amount when it came to writing detective stories, but scarcely any for the practice of medicine.

We will first describe some helpful techniques for concentrating in spite of distractions, then discuss that priceless asset, the will-to-work.

II

Turn your back to the distractions. Booth Tarkington, another famous author, deliberately faced a bare wall when he worked, turning his back to the window and wall decorations that might tempt his mind to wander. He also favored working late at night after others had gone to bed and would not be interrupting him or making distracting noises.

Thomas Jefferson turned his back to the distractions from his many house guests—sometimes fifty of them—at Monticello by going to his poplar grove to work. Impolite, perhaps, but efficient.

Geegaws and mementos that decorate a desk top are often distracting. Try putting them out of sight for a few days and see if it becomes easier to keep your mind on what you should be doing. That pretty-girl calendar, too. It is a good policy to have in view only the articles that are needed for working on the particular job you are doing. Then everything you look at helps draw your wandering thoughts back to the work.

When people are crowded close together, or face each other to save floor space, they are likely to be mutually distracting. Some production lines use plywood dividers between adjacent or facing bench workers; the dividers are just high enough to cut off this source of distraction. A private workplace is likely to be least distracting, even if it is only pseudo-private, as with these dividers.

III

Start work forcefully, don't dillydally when getting under way. People are particularly prone to distractions at the beginning of any task. After being at it for, say, fifteen minutes you become warmed up to the task and it is easier to concentrate on it. A forceful start can take the place of the usual slow warming up. Get down to business right away; no fiddling around or procrastinating.

It helps keep attention on the business at hand if your forceful start includes sitting or standing a bit more erect than usual. An alert posture, no slouching. The little extra muscular tension keeps thoughts on the work better. After you are "in the swing" of the work, ease off the tension if you wish. Tense at the start, relax later.

IV

Start with an enthusiastic, pleasant attitude. Not an "Oh, hum" attitude. Don't start out feeling bored by the prospect of what you have to do; get bored later in the day if you must.

In case you aren't bubbling with spontaneous enthusiasm for what you have to do, then pretend you are and tackle it forcefully. It may seem silly, but pretended enthusiasm does help. We should be thankful that it does, because we often have to do things that do not arouse our spontaneous zest.

Don't wait for enthusiasm to come of its own accord. It may not put in an appearance. But do act as if you were enthusiastic about it.

V

Do first the task or detail you are least enthusiastic about. Start with the hard task, not the easy one. Start with the most distasteful task, not the one you enjoy most. Get these out of the way—and with heaps of pretended enthusiasm—so they are not hanging over your head to haunt you and distract your thoughts.

Unpleasant tasks are powerful distracters until they are completed and can be dropped from mind. By the way, what is the distasteful task you have been putting off?

VI

Keep tabs on how much you get done each hour. This makes work seem more like a game, with a score coming up every hour. Most people who keep tabs find it easier to keep their minds on their work, and they also find that they try to get a little more done each succeeding hour—less likely to distract themselves by mind wandering.

Setting a quota to get so much done in an hour, is a relative of the above. If those students who were supposedly studying in the library had set quotas to study thirty pages an hour they would not have had nearly so many self-distractions.

Budgeting your time, as Thomas Jefferson began to do when he was sixteen, is another relative of keeping tabs. It usually helps one to rise above environmental distractions and temptations toward mind wandering. Planned, rather than planless.

Practical tests have demonstrated that it is more effective to keep tabs, or have quotas, or budget time on an hourly basis rather than daily or weekly. Close-at-hands goals—every hour—have more immediate motivating power than faraway goals.

In addition, when you near a goal there is a *goal gradient spurt* in your work—a "homestretch effect" when you knuckle down to business a little more diligently. Hourly goals, or keeping tabs every hour, encourages this spurt every hour instead of once a day—or none a day if the person has no personal goals set in the work.

Faraway goals can be broken down into close-at-hand hourly goals.

The faraway goal to finish a home-study course in accounting can be broken into the immediate goal of getting one assignment done each evening. Or the goal for the day's output can be broken into hourly quotas; supplies can be stacked in hourly batches rather than for the entire day. Girls who were doing the monotonous work of addressing envelopes by hand, for instance, found it easier to work, and they turned out more, when they were given batches of only 250 envelopes at a time. The last 25 of each batch were addressed more rapidly than the first 25 owing to the goal-gradient effect.

It is easier to set hourly goals, or keep hourly tabs, for some kinds of work than others. For increasing personal efficiency, however, it is worth figuring out some way of setting up an hourly target to aim for. In some work, such as the executive's or housewife's, it may be a sequence of goals or *deadlines*. For instance, to finish studying the divisional reports by nine-thirty, to have all important letters dictated by ten-thirty, conferences on promotions finished by eleven-thirty, and so on.

Be realistic in setting hourly goals or deadlines. Don't make them so easy that you can putter away much of the hour. And don't make them so difficult that you cannot achieve them, for this is disheartening rather than encouraging. They should be stiff enough to prompt you to start forcefully and to make you keep your mind on your work.

A good basis for setting them is to make them just a little stiffer than you have been doing in the past. And when you reach this goal you can again make it a little stiffer. Progress in personal efficiency.

Until you prod yourself by realistic hourly quotas you have set for yourself you will never know how well you can make your mind stay put and work despite hindrances. Sir Arthur Conan Doyle had quotas—deadlines—to help him keep his mind on his work; he had to finish a story a week for the *Strand* magazine.

VII

We are more creatures of habit than we sometimes like to admit. Some of the habits are strengths, others not. It is a weakness if one has the habit of being easily distracted. But it is often possible to form habits in the other direction, of concentrating despite difficulties in the way.

This often happens with a young person just starting work in a distracting office or factory. The first few days, or weeks, he is readily distracted by all that is going on around him in that strange new world. But as he "gets used to" the noises and movements that first

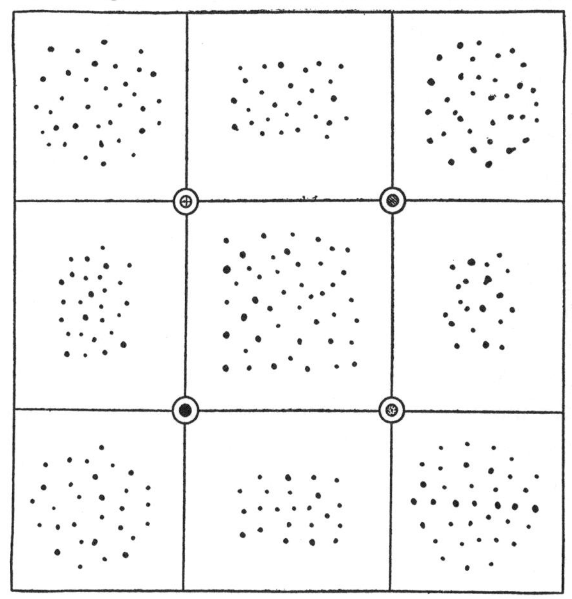

41. COUNT THE DOTS FOR PRACTICE IN CONCENTRATING

Without pointing a finger or pencil, count the dots in each square and keep a record of the number you count in each separate square. Keep the record on a separate sheet of paper and out of sight.

The next day turn the book one-fourth of the way around and count the dots again. Keep a record of the number you counted on another separate sheet of paper. Do not compare the count with the first day's count yet.

The third day turn the book another one-fourth way around and repeat the counting and record keeping.

On the fourth day, after counting without pointing use a pencil and make a careful count of the exact number of dots. Compare this with the counts you made on the unaided days. Did your count become more accurate day after day?

distracted him he pays less and less attention to them and acquires the *habit of concentrating* (more or less!) amidst the confusion.

By starting forcefully, and keeping hourly tabs, you can help build that habit so it is more rather than less. On the theory that the habit of concentrating is formed best by intentionally concentrating, some clinical psychologists recommend special practice sessions for scatterbrained people.

Practice in mental arithmetic is one exercise they use. Start with any number under ten, add seven to it, and keep on adding seven to each successive total until 1,000 is reached. If that requires too much concentration the first time you try it, make it easier by speaking the successive totals aloud. After a few trials you will be able to do it silently, entirely in your head. Start with a different number each time. To break the monotony, you can add eight's or nine's for a change—and you can also pretend it is fun.

(Some people have practiced multiplying three-place numbers by three-place numbers—742 x 638—entirely in their heads, and have reached the point where they could do it for twelve hours a day!)

Practice working against distracting sounds for another training exercise. Turn the radio on softly to some dramatic or news broadcast (not music), and work some variation of that mental arithmetic, or try memorizing a poem silently.

Practice shadowing some stranger for fifteen minutes on a busy street, not losing sight of him. This is the easiest of the exercises, since it is almost a game. Take a tip from that and try to make a game of more of the things you do.

VIII

Regular times and places for work make concentration less of a problem—another aspect of helpful habits.

The helpfulness in this instance is mostly owing to the mental set which the regular time and place arouse. If you lounge in a favorite chair in front of television, for instance, you just naturally have a mental set for being entertained, not of concentrating on an analysis of the day's stock-market movements. Children can keep their minds on their homework better when they have special chairs and tables for homework use only and set hours for starting it.

A workplace should be used for work only. If you eat lunch, visit, or sleep there, the surroundings may give you a mental set for visiting when it should be for working.

IX

A well-developed *will-to-work* is probably the greatest asset one can have to get things done in spite of hindrances and for personal efficiency in general. The person with a strong will-to-work is persevering instead of quitting, enthusiastic instead of apathetic, industrious rather than indolent, doing instead of excusing.

The will-to-work does not seem to be an inborn propensity or instinct. The most thorough search for such a propensity has been made by Dr. Raymond B. Cattell, using factor-analysis methods which reveal the basic or unitary human traits. He has found a dozen propensities but only the barest suggestion that a will-to-work might be a common inborn characteristic of humans.

How do people get a will-to-work? Do they get it because they have to work to make a living? No, for some of the world's most diligent workers have been rich men. Here are a few of the rich men who worked like beavers and advanced the world thereby:

ARISTOTLE, philosopher and scientist of the Golden Age of ancient Greece.
COUNT GEORGES BUFFON, author of forty-four ponderous volumes on natural science.
HENRY CAVENDISH, richest man in England, who turned his mansion into a library and laboratory for chemical discoveries.
CHARLES DARWIN, the easily-tired man who devoted his life to the study of evolution.
ANTOINE LAVOISIER, founder of modern chemistry who started work at 6 A.M. to get more done.
MARCHESE GUGLIELMO MARCONI, inventor of wireless telegraphy.
WILLIAM H. PRESCOTT, blind authority on the history of Spain and Mexico.
HEINRICH SCHLIEMANN, self-taught archaeologist who located and excavated the ruins of ancient Troy.
FREDERICK W. TAYLOR, founder of scientific management.

Those men did not work to make a living or to make money. Most of them poured their fortunes into their work. They were working for more than money—at work that (a) challenged them, (b) interested them, and (c) gave them a feeling of accomplishment. Those are apparently essential ingredients in the will-to-work: challenge, interest, accomplishment.

Those three ingredients gave those men a strong mental set for their work. Their work was uppermost in their minds at most times and most places. They had no need to pretend enthusiasm when starting out each morning. They plunged in forcefully, eagerly, without trying.

But note this—most of them did not have a strong will-to-work until they happened to find the kind of work that challenged, interested, and gave them a feeling of doing something worth while. That touched off the "divine spark."

Charles Darwin's father, for instance, sent him to medical school; the son wanted to study natural science and couldn't keep his mind on the medical courses, so he failed. Then his father sent him to

42. Inheriting a nice job may undermine the will to work. (From booklet "Growing Pains;" Courtesy The Connecticut Mutual Life Insurance Company)

theological school, and that was still worse on the son's will-to-work; Charles played hookey from classes to roam the countryside collecting specimens. His father gave up, allowed the son to follow his bent in nature study, but warned the boy that nature study did not amount to anything and that he would be a failure. The father underestimated what the divine spark of a will-to-work can accomplish.

Despite Darwin's overpowering will-to-work at nature study he still set up a time schedule which he rigidly followed for more than forty years. It kept him at work systematically, rather than by fits and starts. He scheduled work for every day in the week, including

Sundays. His daily time budget included periods for answering mail, taking exercise, playing with his children, and religious devotions. But first of all on each day's schedule he put his painstaking work in his self-chosen field of science.

Nowadays it is not always possible to choose exactly the kind of work one might prefer. Most people work for companies, where a large share of jobs are simplified and not especially challenging. Work has been planned by others and may not be of much intrinsic interest to the individual worker. It may be boresome, in fact, but necessary in order to make a living. When that is the situation, the will-to-work is likely to wither away; not much thought about efficient working, and thoughts are easily distracted from the work. That is why it is so essential for perhaps the majority of employed people, and some reluctant housewives, to train themselves to make systematic daily use of the techniques we have given.

If a person has too strong a will-to-work is he likely to overwork and undermine his well-being? The next chapter takes up that question, and the answer may amaze you.

17. How Hard Is It Safe to Work?

I

HOW HARD AND HOW LONG CAN A PERSON SAFELY WORK WITHOUT resting? How long should one rest after twenty minutes of really hard labor?

The answers to those questions need no longer be learned the hard way. Research in the United States Air Force School of Aviation Medicine now provides a guide for grading work according to its severity. We will summarize what Drs. J. Gordon Wells and Bruno Balke found, and also illustrate the hardness of work by various tasks which have been reported on by other researchers. These everyday tasks will help you keep an eye on your own working efficiency.

The Air Force research was done on men ranging from twenty-two to forty-seven years of age. They were in good health, and much more hardened to heavy work than the average person is; hardened enough so that they could keep going when most of us would have to stop to rest.

The work they were tested with was simple—merely walk on a treadmill at the moderate gait of three and one half miles per hour. When they started the walk the treadmill was level, walking was easy. But the experimenters made it harder each minute by raising the far end of the treadmill steadily. After twenty minutes of work the men were thus climbing up a steep grade of 20 per cent—really hard walking. (The steepness of the grade gave a basis for computing the foot-pounds of work the men did each minute.)

As the men climbed this adjustable hill, the doctors were getting records of their pulse rate, blood pressure, breathing rate, amount of air breathed, oxygen used, and lactic acid (lactate) in the blood.

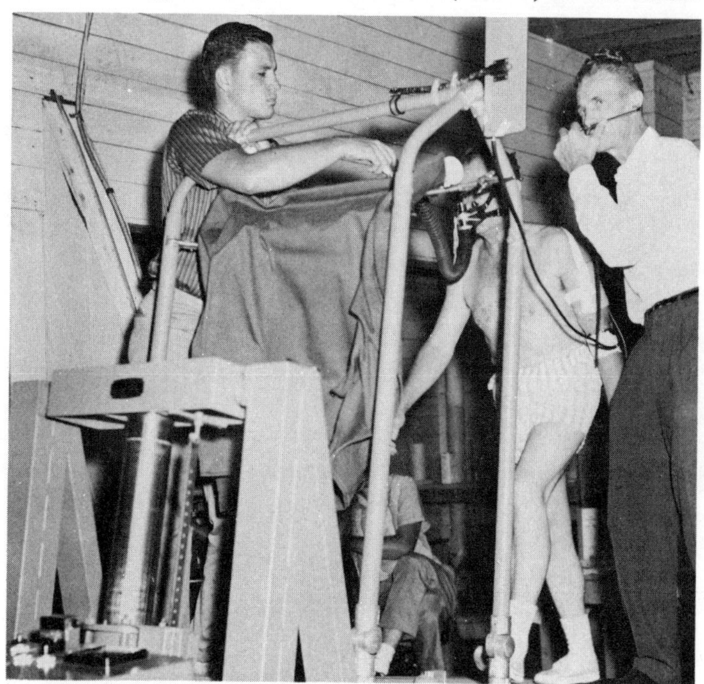

43. MEASURING WORK CAPACITY ON THE "ADJUSTABLE HILL"

This motor driven treadmill keeps the man walking at a steady pace of 3.4 miles an hour. It is level when he starts, but the walking is gradually made more taxing by the treadmill slope being increased by 1 per cent each succeeding minute by the hydraulic piston seen in the lower left. As the man walks up this steadily increasing grade Dr. Bruno Balke is measuring his pulse rate and blood pressure. The walker breathes through a large tube connected to apparatus for measuring his volume of breathing and oxygen consumption. The walking is stopped when heart or breathing perfomance indicate he is at the limit of his capacities. In this picture the test was stopped after 17 minutes of walking on the 17 per cent upgrade, when the man's crest load had been reached. The treadmill is at 17 per cent slope in this picture. (Photo by J. D. Allred. Courtesy the U.S. Civil Aeromedical Research Institute)

II

The researchers were especially interested in the lactate because when any muscle contracts some of the tiny amount of glycogen (blood sugar) in it is used as fuel and lactate is left behind from the glycogen. The amount of lactate in the blood rises slightly when heavier work is started, but usually goes back to normal within a few minutes, as the next paragraph describes. Light work, little lactate; heavy work, more lactate at the end of a minute.

One of the body's daily miracles is the way it turns about four-fifths of the lactate back into glycogen rather promptly when conditions are favorable. Thus it is used as fuel over and over again, although with a little loss each time.

Imagine an automobile that could turn a large part of its exhaust back into high-octane gasoline! Yet our bodies do a comparable job all the time. A marvel that helps human efficiency greatly.

But there is a limitation to this daily marvel. As work becomes heavier, the lactate is produced in greater amounts than the blood and breathing can bring oxygen to synthesize the lactate back into glycogen promptly. Then some of the lactate accumulates.

The tests on that adjustable hill showed how rapidly, and how much, the lactate accumulated. Each time the hill was made 1 per cent steeper there was an increase in the lactate.

III

When the hill was only 3 to 4 per cent steep, the lactate did not increase enough to matter. Although that was a gentle climb, the men were nevertheless really working. That was shown by their pulse rates which went up to 120 a minute. Their systolic blood pressure also rose 20 points higher than when they were walking on the level. They were also using about four times as much oxygen as when standing still. (The aisle in most church and theater auditoriums is at least that steep—reason enough for some people to be out of breath on leaving the auditorium.

But as the hill was made steeper than that, lactate was produced in accelerated amounts. By the time the men came to climb the 20 per cent grade, the lactate was almost six times what it had been when standing at rest.

And on that final 20 per cent climb—like going up some of San Francisco's hills—the pulse rate rose to 190 a minute. The men were also breathing more than three times as rapidly, and breathing about ten times more air a minute, and their systolic blood pressure was 70 points higher than at the start. They were also using more than four times as much oxygen as when they began the climb of a 1 per cent grade.

It had been truly exhausting work, although it lasted only twenty minutes, and the steepest climb had taken only one minute.

Better rest when you get to the top of that steep hill, if not before you reach the top.

IV

After twenty minutes of that kind of work, how long did the men need to rest to restore their bodily condition to a normal resting, steady state?

After five minutes' rest their pulse rates had dropped to 117 a minute—still above the "safety limit" of 110.

But the lactate had actually increased in their blood during the five-minute rest! How is that possible? Partly because their muscles had produced lactate more rapidly during the hard part of the climb than the blood could take it away. Toward the end of the work their muscles had, so to speak, been lactate logged.

Not only lactate logged, but as soon as the men started to rest their circulation slowed down tremendously—from 190 beats a minute to 117 in five minutes. The slowed circulation brought much less oxygen to the muscles than was demanded to synthesize four-fifths of the lactate back into glycogen.

Five minutes of fairly complete rest thus did not help them much. It would have helped more, as other experiments show, if the men had moved around enough during the rest to keep their circulation bringing enough oxygen to where it was desperately needed.

All this leads to two practical guides to follow when doing heavy muscular work, and by heavy we mean heavier than you have been used to doing, not necessarily climbing up a 20 per cent grade:

Take a rest, or make a marked change of pace, after even a short bout of exertion that makes you breathe more than usual, or that makes your heart beat faster than the "safety limit."

Your muscle efficiency will recover more rapidly if you engage in some moderate activity rather than lying motionless during the rest period.

V

How heavy does a task have to be to bring about an efficiency-lowering accumulation of lactates?

And how do various tasks rank in heaviness? Which is heavier labor, scrubbing the floor on all fours, or walking at a speed of four miles an hour?

On the basis of their findings, Drs. Wells and Balke made this six-step classification of the severity of work:

1. Mild
2. Moderate
3. OPTIMAL ← Optimal uses about half the capacity the average adult has for physical work. It does not deplete the energy of an adult in good condition.
4. Strenuous
5. Maximal
6. Exhausting

Now for a close-up of each of those levels of work.

1. *Mild work*

Pulse remains under	100 per minute
Breathing per minute	14 or less
Calories used per minute	4 or less
Foot-pounds of work per minute	1,000 or less
Lactate	No accumulation

Mild work can safely be kept up indefinitely by people who are not too sedentary. The only need for rest pauses, or to change pace, is to break the monotony or boredom.

The following tasks require four calories or less per minute for the average person, and are arranged with the mildest at the top of the list. (It takes from one to one and one half calories per minute for the average person to sit or stand, doing no visible work.)

Clerical
Typing
Cooking
Home ironing
Home sewing
Light assembly work
Tailoring
Walking two miles per hour on level

Setting up exercises
Washing windows
Dusting
Mopping
Driving truck (not loading it)
Making beds

2. *Moderate work*

Pulse remains under	120 per minute
Breathing per minute	15 or less
Calories used per minute	5 to 8
Foot-pounds of work per minute	4,000 or less
Lactate	No significant accumulation

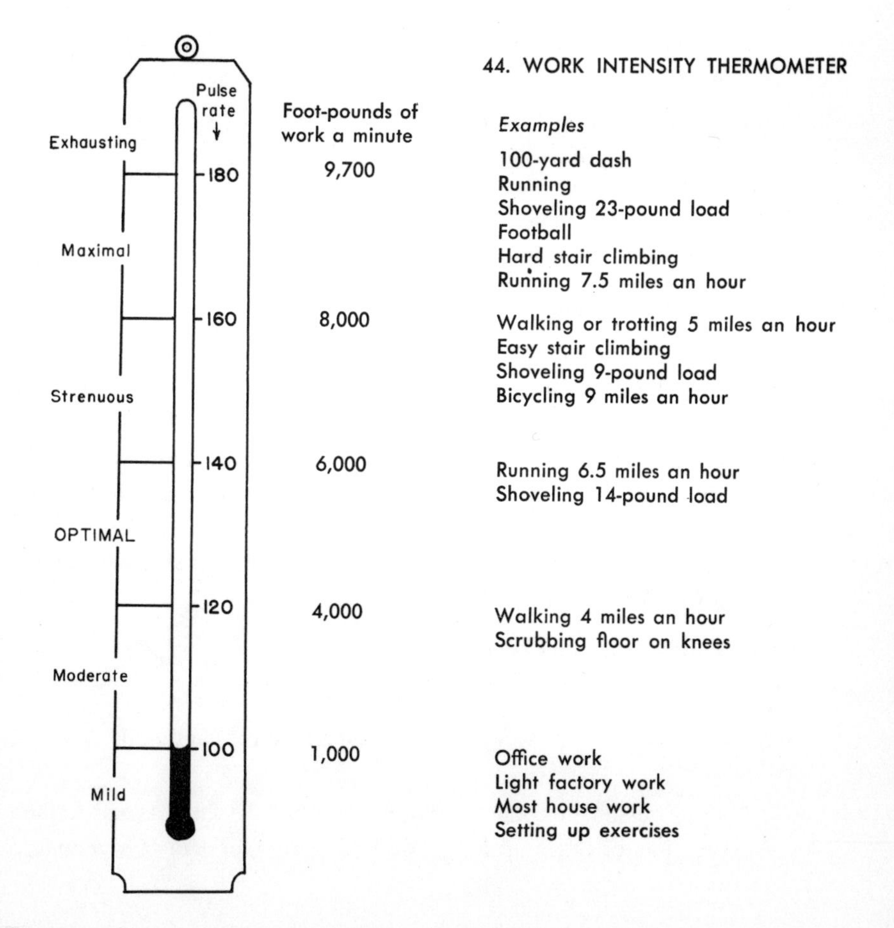

44. WORK INTENSITY THERMOMETER

Moderate work can be kept up eight hours daily on the job by people who are used to it. Rest pauses are needed only because of boredom or poor condition (sedentariness), or for spurts of heavier work, or because the same few muscles are used over and over again, as in folding handkerchiefs.

Examples of moderate work, with the tasks using fewer calories at the top:

Scrubbing floor on knees
Making beds
Assembling parts weighing 25 pounds
Hand printing
Walking four miles per hour on level

People are usually astonished when they first learn that some of those tasks are not heavy work. The body is more efficient than these people give it credit for.

3. *OPTIMAL work*

Pulse remains under	140 per minute
Breathing per minute	16 or less
Calories used per minute	9 to 10
Foot-pounds of work per minute	6,000 or less
Lactate in blood	2 times resting quantity
Systolic blood pressure	40 points higher than resting

Rest pauses are a physiological necessity when optimal work is being done. Yet with suitable rest pauses a person *in good condition* can safely keep it up for an eight-hour day. But the sedentary person should not try optimal work for more than a few minutes a day. If you are sedentary, it will require two or three months of progressive conditioning exercises to get you into shape.

Some tasks which are of this level, with the one using fewest calories at the top of the list are the following:

Bicycle riding nine miles per hour
Shoveling nine pound load (dry snow, for instance)
Easy stair climbing
Walking three and one-half miles per hour up 10 per cent grade
Hand riveting

Only a person in good condition, it should be emphasized again, can keep any of those up long. Dr. Balke, an expert in biodynamics, told us, "unfortunately, about three-fourths of our male population approach complete exhaustion after one to three hours walking up a 10 per cent hill."

4. *Strenuous work*

Pulse remains under	160 per minute
Breathing per minute	20 or less
Calories used per minute	11 to 12
Foot-pounds of work per minute	8,000 or less
Lactate in blood	2½ times resting quantity
Systolic blood pressure	55 points higher than resting

Strenuous work requires more and longer rest pauses, even for a person in good condition. It should not be tried by a sedentary person for more than a minute or two a day. Examples:

Skiing on level, three and one-half miles an hour, no load carried
Shoveling 14-pound loads
Walking five miles per hour on level
Running five and one-half miles an hour on level
Loading (100-pound loads)
Blacksmithing
Rowing boat three and one-half miles an hour

5. *Maximal work*

Pulse remains under	180 per minute
Breathing per minute	25 or less
Calories used per minute	13 to 15
Foot-pounds of work per minute	9,700 or less
Lactate in blood	5 times resting amount
Systolic blood pressure	65 points above resting

Work of this intensity is only for those in especially good condition, and they should do it only on scattered occasions, regardless of how young they are. The well-conditioned man of fifty to sixty can do it safely; the sedentary youth better not try. Even the well-conditioned cannot do it long, because his blood quickly gets five times the amount of resting lactate and the machine simply stalls. Examples:

Skiing on level, three and one-half miles an hour, carrying 20-pound load
College football
Hard stair climbing
Skiing on level, three and one-half miles an hour, carrying 30-pound load

6. *Exhausting work*

Pulse around	180 or higher
Breathing per minute	26 or higher
Calories used per minute	16 or higher
Foot-pounds of work per minute	10,200 or higher
Lactate in blood	6 or more times resting
Systolic blood pressure	65 or more points above resting

This work, too, is only for the sturdy and hardened persons. Even they can keep at it only a few minutes at a time, and sometimes collapse in the midst of it. Examples:

Swimming 120 feet per minute
Shoveling 23-pound load (such as wet snow)
Running 100-yard dash
Collegiate wrestling
Crew rowing

VI

Those lists of progressively taxing activities reflect some significant tendencies.

One is that it should be easy to be efficient at most white-collar work.

Another is that the really hard activities are almost all done "for fun." And because they are done for fun, many people neglect to take the rest pauses they may need desperately.

Another is that if typing or sewing or other mild tasks could be as much fun as rowing a boat or skiing, the person would never need a rest pause. But, alas! the mild tasks one does to make a living are seldom as engrossing as sports, so the person needs a rest although his muscles do not.

18. The Law of Heavy Laboring

I

WHY SHOULD WE BE CONCERNED ABOUT HEAVY LABORING THESE days?

It is true that much heavy laboring is now done for us by electricity, gasoline, and diesel oil power. But heavy laboring has not been eliminated, as your occasional sore muscles and getting out of breath testify. Snow still has to be shoveled by hand, gardens spaded, furniture moved around, youngsters lifted, and 20-pound bags of groceries carried from the supermarket.

And strange as it may seem, we are more vulnerable to heavy laboring because we do so little of it. This is because people become "out of condition," as the athletic coach calls it, when they do not do heavy work fairly regularly. Today practically all white-collar people, and a large share of blue-collar people, are sedentary, or out of condition, for even moderate physical work.

As a result of their sedentariness their muscles are below what they might be in both strength and in staying power.

In addition, most of the sedentary person's vital processes slump to a low level. When he walks from the parking lot to his office, for instance, a sedentary man uses up about 10 per cent more oxygen than one who has been used to hard laboring and whose organs consequently operate at a higher level of physiological efficiency. When the sedentary person climbs stairs his heart speeds up much more than the nonsedentary person's.

The widespread sedentary condition is thus the reason why most people lose their breath when they carry the weekly groceries. (Thomas Jefferson would have recommended using a two-wheeled cart for greater efficiency in carrying groceries.) It is also the sedentary person who is most likely to topple over with a heart attack while shoveling snow, especially when the snow is wet and heavy. These people are especially vulnerable to strenuous exertion and should carefully follow all the guides for heavy laboring.

II

How was the "Law of Heavy Laboring" discovered?

Frederick W. Taylor, the father of scientific management, was the first person to make a thorough study of heavy laboring. He may have had a personal interest in this, because he disliked physical work though he did it conscientiously when necessary. Companies were also interested because there was a great amount of heavy work to be done by man power alone, until after World War I. Unskilled labor—muscle power—was used in great quantities, and although the rate of pay was the lowest, it added up to sizable totals in a firm's costs.

For example, at the steel mill where the work we will describe was done there was an average of 500 laborers working in the yard each day. They did nothing but carry, lift, or shovel all week long. The yard stretched for two miles along the river and averaged about a half-mile wide. Great piles of coke, rice coal, sand, ore, and pigs of finished iron dotted the area.

Yard laborers were neglected men before Taylor. They still worked the way in which the Egyptians had in building the pyramids—brute force and perspiration.

"Anyone knows how to carry or shovel," was the prevailing belief. "An idiot or gorilla can do it." So no effort had been made to find whether there might be better ways to carry or shovel. The only attempt at efficiency was for the boss to watch that the men did not loaf on the job.

But Taylor held the deep belief that any work could be done more efficiently, even simple laboring. Anyway, it made his back ache just to watch the men carry pigs of iron. Taylor could work all day at a lathe and feel fresh as a daisy at quitting time, but that was moderate to mild work in comparison with yard laboring; much of the time at a lathe was spent merely standing and watching, which gave Taylor many minutes to rest while the machines were doing the work.

When he proposed to improve the manual laborers' efficiency his closest associates tried to head him off. The associate he listened to most, pint-sized Carl G. Barth, a mathematical genius, even quoted the laws of thermodynamics to "prove" that the efficiency of heavy laboring could not be improved. That was a challenge to Taylor to get to the root of the matter.

So Taylor made one experiment, and apparently it showed nothing. Then another, then a third, which merely seemed to confuse them further. But they kept going back to the records of these experiments, trying to discover some key that would explain the results. Finally excitable Barth hit upon an algebraic formula for work that consists of recurring cycles of the same activity. This at last made sense of their experimental records. When he rushed to explain it to Taylor he was so excited that he forgot to use his usual cuss words.

What he explained was called the "Law of Heavy Laboring," or sometimes the "Law of Endurance." It states that muscles can function efficiently at recurring activity when they are under load for only a part of the time, the length of the time depending upon the size of the load. For carrying 90-pound loads, for example, they calculated that the man's arm should be under load only 43 per cent of the time. For a 45-pound load the efficient working phase went up to only 58 per cent of the time. (Their figures applied, of course, to men who were accustomed to heavy labor, who were not sedentary—imagine a sedentary office clerk lifting a 90-pound filing cabinet off the floor!)

They found that it was heavy laboring just to stand motionless, like Atlas, and hold the load—as some housewives learn when they have their arms full of groceries or babies and stop to visit.

III

Did this law improve efficiency when it was applied?

Opposition to trying out that "Law of Heavy Laboring" on a large scale weakened when the Spanish-American War erupted. The steel mill had 80,000 tons of pig iron piled around the yard. The war increased the demand for pig iron so that there was a rush job loading it into freight cars. This gave Taylor a chance to test the law.

Each pig of iron weighed 92 pounds; no doubt of it being heavy labor. The worker would pick up a pig, his hands protected by wide leather straps, carry it up inclined planks, and drop it into a gondola freight car. The walk averaged only thirty-six feet to the car. But

—Courtesy "Banter" of Colgate University.

Terrible Predicament of the Industrial Psychologist Who Lost His Whistle After Blowing for the Rest Period.

during a day a worker walked a total of eight miles while carrying ninety-two pounds, and another eight miles returning with empty hands. The average laborer had been loading 12½ long tons of iron a day.

The empty-handed return trip was not heavy laboring, except for "holding back" when walking down the planks. The men's arms were under load about 50 per cent of the time. But the law stated that efficiency was lowered if the arms were under a load that size more than 43 per cent of the workday. Here was an opportunity to check the validity of the new law by cutting down the time the men were under load to 43 per cent and see if their efficiency did increase.

After the president gave his reluctant approval to try it out, Taylor worked out a schedule of rest periods and detailed a special supervisor to enforce the schedule. After walking the plank from ten to twenty times the men were to rest. They were also told to drop, not throw, the pig into the car, because throwing was heavy work.

The length of the rests was systematically varied during the day. There were ten-minute, two-minute, fifteen-minute, and three-minute rests peppered through the day. The average was three minutes' rest after carrying for twelve minutes—20 per cent of the time resting.

This new mixture of rest with heavy labor was tried out first on a one hundred and thirty-pound Pennsylvania Dutchmen; not large, but wiry and hardened by years of laboring—far from sedentary. Heavy laboring apparently had not tired him excessively because at closing whistle he hurried home at a dog trot to work at building his house until darkness fell.

Such a "tireless laborer" would be a severe test of the new law. But when he was put on the systematic rest schedule he was soon carrying an average of 47 tons a day and still trotting home for his do-it-yourself housebuilding. And as other laborers were put on the new schedule they, too, were soon carrying almost four times as much as previously each day.

IV

Do systematic rest pauses always give such large increases in efficiency?

They should always give a worth-while increase when heavy physical work is done, but there are two reasons why they do not always. Sometimes they fail to improve efficiency because the pauses are too long, or too short, or are not taken at the proper times, or are not spent in restful ways. Sometimes they fail because the person does not want to improve and, either deliberately or unintentionally, achieves far below what he might.

Taylor was lucky on both scores. He "hit it on the nose" when he worked out the rest schedules, and was especially careful in advance to win the men's cooperation and have their will-to-work.

It is now known that suitable rest pauses will also bring increased efficiency in light work that is continuous; light day-long tasks such as typing or folding handkerchiefs are almost always benefited. Since easy work also benefits, obviously some things in addition to the "Law of Heavy Laboring" have to be considered. Boredom and monotony, particularly. As a general *guide,* whenever anything is done for an hour or longer, no matter how light and easy it may seem, efficiency can almost always be boosted by suitable rest pauses.

V

Is it actually possible for a person to lift as much as 47 tons a day?

That does seem to most white-collar people to be a superhuman amount of work, but they underestimate how much can be done by people who are in condition for doing manual work. Many white-collar people could do that much themselves by gradually getting into condition and also by using the techniques, or tricks, which make it easier to handle heavy loads.

Consider the daily lifting done by James Russell Lowell, the poet, who was of medium height, rather slender, but sinewy and active as a result of his lifting. He began this lifting when he was twenty-six and doing the sedentary work of editing. He hoped the lifting would give him "a wholesome appearance of health and good spirits."

Each morning he lifted a pair of 24-pound dumbbells 300 times as an eye opener and pepper-upper. Multiply 300 by 24 pounds and you will find that each hand lifted 3 2/10 long tons before breakfast —a total of nearly six and one-half tons for both hands.

Again at evening he lifted the weights another three hundred times, making the day's total nearly thirteen long tons.

Easy for the freckled poet with the wavy hair, after he got used to it. But we can be sure that the first time he tried it he was probably out of breath after a dozen lifts because his capacity for lifting was then underdeveloped. It was his writing, such as "The Vision of Sir Launfal," not his weight lifting, that gained him a niche in the American Hall of Fame. People should know about his 13 tons daily, however, because it illustrates the surprising capacity people can develop for heavy laboring.

The pig-iron carriers had developed and were using that capacity almost to the full; most of us seldom do, so we remain in doubt about what we could do. The 47 tons a day the yard laborers were finally carrying was just about the upper limit for steady heavy work, as was shown in the preceding chapter. They were helped in their work by having learned some tricks that made the work less strenuous than it would otherwise have been. In the next chapter we will take up the techniques which can make heavy laboring a little lighter, following which we will take up the fine points which make rest pauses more beneficial than they often are.

19. Efficient Lifting, Carrying, and Shoveling

I

NO MATTER HOW EASY OUR REGULAR WORK MAY BE, OR HOW MECHanized our homes, there are occasions when we have to stretch ourselves to lift, carry, shovel, or dig. In these sedentary times we probably should do more of such work to raise our strength and staying power. But unless we do these strenuous tasks properly, instead of benefiting we can injure our backs, get sore muscles, bring on heart attacks, or—most likely—get "pooped out" quickly and be in no shape for work the rest of the day.

It's smart to know—and diligently use—the techniques which enable us to lift or carry loads with the least exertion. There have been many laboratory investigations made of this, and there is a great amount that has been learned the hard way, in the School of Experience.

As you study the techniques we will describe for efficient *lifting* you will notice that most of them take advantage of the leverage provided by the way joints and muscles are arranged. When you understand how to use muscles as physical levers to best advantage, then loads can be handled which you could not budge otherwise. For one example in advance, an arm that can lift only 26 pounds when the arm is in one position can lift 40 pounds if its position is changed to use its leverage—55 per cent more "strength" by using leverage that is built into the body.

Since this leverage is ordinarily not used intentionally, most people underestimate how much they could lift or carry, so do not get the thrill of finding out how much capacity they have for physical work. Now for some *lifting guides.*

1. Stand as close as possible to the heavy object you want to lift, feet touching it—but not under it, just in case it might fall.

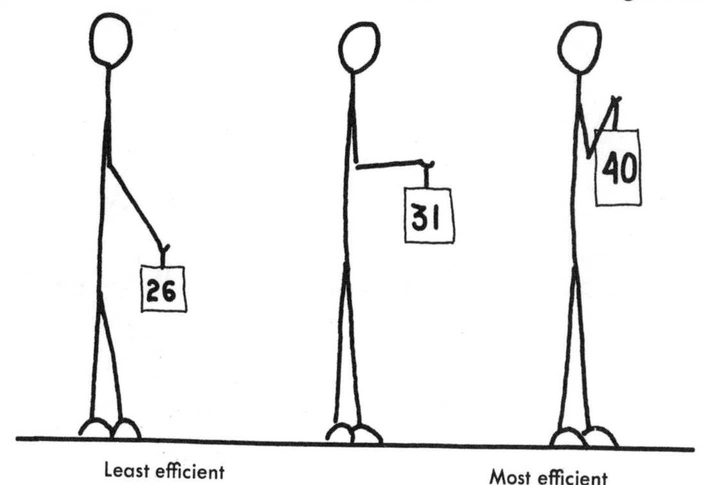

Numerals show the number of pounds the average person can lift with one hand when the elbow is in the angle illustrated

46. HOW THE ELBOW ANGLE AFFECTS LIFTING AND CARRYING

Standing close is essential because the arms have only a little lifting leverage (or strength) when stretched out in front, and practically none when stretched out at the sides. The leverage is much greater when we use the elbow joint rather than the shoulder joint. Demonstrate this to yourself by lifting a thick mail-order catalogue with one hand, using the elbow joint only, then the shoulder joint only; it's hard work when you keep the elbow straight and use only the shoulder.

A similar principle applies to the legs. Use the more powerful leverage of the knee joint in preference to the hip joint. To get up from a chair, for instance, pull one foot back so its heel is even with the front edge of the seat. Pull the other foot a little farther back. Now lean forward slightly and at the same time raise yourself easily and gracefully to a standing position by mostly knee power. No writhing, struggling, or boosting by arms.

2. When a weight is about the limit you can handle, use both hands to lift one end of it first. Lift it high enough to slip one hand under to hold that end. Then quickly slip the other hand under the other end. Now lift with both hands. Try lifting a full-size typewriter or similar weight by this method to demonstrate how much more efficiently it can be lifted.

Least efficient
—feet too far away
—back will do too much of the lifting

More efficient
—feet close to object
—legs do the lifting
—hands should be under the object if it is heavy

47. STAND CLOSE TO LIFT EFFICIENTLY

3. Put in a little extra exertion at the start, but never jerk. A jerk may tear or rupture a muscle. A contracted muscle, however, is less likely to tear than a relaxed muscle. Apply that fact and contract the lifting muscles for a few seconds to "get ready" before you give the mighty heave that lifts the object. Always take up the slack before you push or pull. If you can't budge it without jerking, get someone to help you—don't try to be a superman.

4. Keep the palms of your hands turned upward whenever the shape of the object permits. When the palm is downward the powerful biceps muscle is almost powerless. The average arm can lift 10 pounds more when its palm is turned upward—that makes 20 pounds more when both hands can be used palm upward. Hands under it and palms up. Get under things; don't try lifting them by squeezing their sides.

5. Lift with your knees—the crouching muscles—not your back.

Knees can exert much more lifting power. In addition, if back muscles are used for heavy or continued lifting the sacroiliac joint or the back may be injured. Take our word for this, don't try to test it out.

When the object is on the ground, lift it with knee power by getting down on one knee, or both knees, depending upon the weight. Kneel, don't stoop. Keep your back vertical. Take hold of the object as instructed in rules 2 and 4, then raise it to about the level of your waist; roll it up your thighs if it is too heavy to lift easily, but be especially careful that you are not using your back muscles. (By the time it's at waist level your arms are in a position to exert about 20 per cent more lift than at ground level.) After the load is at waist

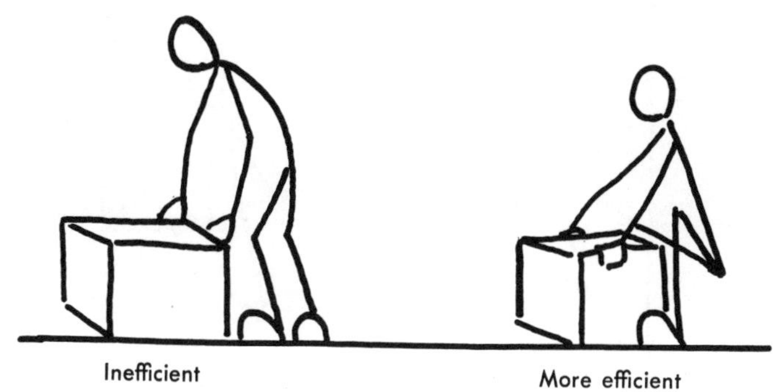

48. CROUCH OR KNEEL TO LIFT EFFICIENTLY

Crouch when the load is light
Kneel on one knee for moderately heavy lifts
On both knees for starting a heavy lift
. . . and get your hands under it

level, straighten your knees, and you are ready to go places with the load. This way you should easily handle that heavy bag of fertilizer or the box containing the big encyclopedia.

When the object is already waist high on a table, or the bag of groceries on the checkout counter at the supermarket, again use the knees rather than the back. Pull the bag close to you—that's rule number 1. Then bend your knees slightly—scrooch—so your hands can slip under the object, palms up. Keep your back vertical and don't stoop. Simply straighten your knees to raise the load. Easy, graceful, and there is less chance that the bottom of the bag will come apart.

6. Keep your elbows close to your sides when lifting. They are not

wings. The muscle force of the arms is less when the elbows are held away from the body like wings. To move a long object, such as a patio bench, don't take hold of the ends; that would cut down your effective strength because your elbows would be away from your sides. The better way is to grasp the long object near its middle, your hands about eighteen inches apart, which will allow your elbows to remain close to your sides. Support your elbows on your hipbones, if you want more stability. Always grasp heavy objects so that your hands are no more than about eighteen nches apart.

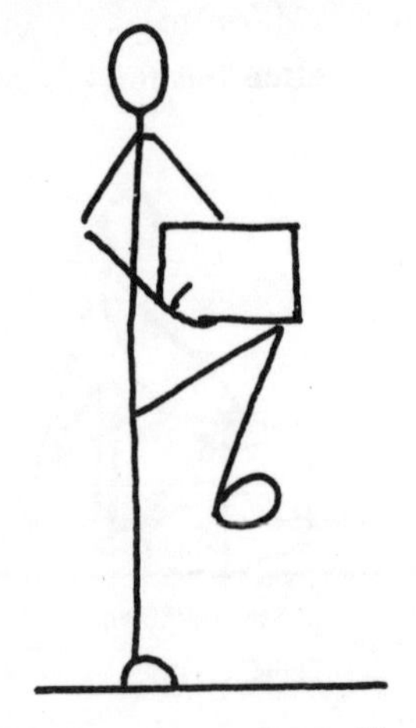

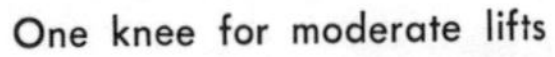

One knee for moderate lifts — Both knees for heavy lifts

49. USE THE KNEES TO HELP LIFT THE LOAD

The knees can help get the load up where the elbow angle gives greater lifting power . . . but watch your balance while doing this

7. Have your elbow joint at right angles when starting to lift—the lower arm at right angles to the upper arm. Arms can lift about 20 per cent more in this position than when the elbow joint is straight. A heavy object you cannot budge with arms straight can often be lifted if you get into a position so you can start with the elbows at right angles and close to your sides. That is one advantage from getting on your knees when lifting from the ground. It is easier to start lifting if the object is on a platform or table that is at least waist high; if higher than that, more efficient, as will appear in a moment.

This rule should also be applied when turning a crank, as in lifting by a hand winch or in cranking a machine. The cranking can be done most efficiently when the center of the crank shaft is about waist high.

8. Grunt! This may seem silly, but it is serious. People tend to hold their breaths while lifting. This compresses the vital organs in the chest and raises blood pressure considerably. (People who have high blood pressure should avoid heavy lifting.) A grunt is guttural breath-

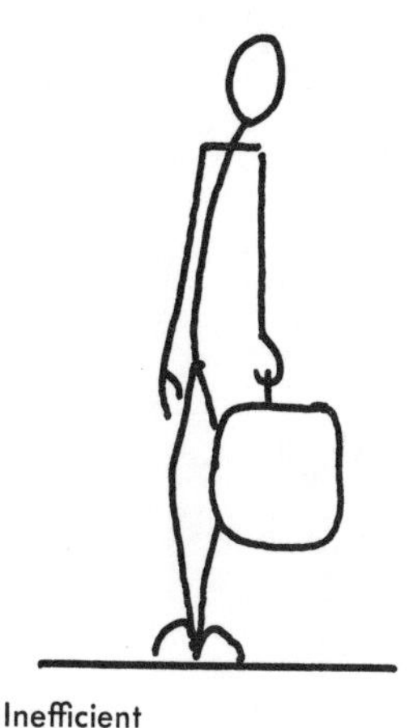

Inefficient
—body pulled to one side
—weak fingers hold the load
—straight arm is weak
. . . he should hold his free arm outward to counterbalance the load

Efficient
—body balanced
—strong forearms hold the load
—arm at right angle is strong

50. EFFICIENT CARRYING

ing that relieves the compression. When you start the mighty heave, grunt but don't jerk. At the supermarket grunting is optimal.

II

Once the load is lifted and securely held, how can we *carry* it most efficiently?

1. Carry the load so that your body posture is interfered with the least. Tests show that carrying a load from a shoulder yoke, as was used by pioneer women, is the most efficient. Next most efficient is to use both hands to hold it close in front of your waist. Carrying on one shoulder is a little less efficient, and also produces back strain. The least efficient is to carry it on one hip.

When a loaded pack is carried on the back, as is done by mountain climbers, it does not make any difference whether it is high or low on the back.

2. Carry it with the hands under it, palms up whenever possible. This is better than using a handle or hugging it. Experienced waiters carry loaded trays with their hands under the tray, not squeezing the rim. Easier to balance the load, too.

3. Carry it with the elbows close to your sides. Remember, your arms have more lift then.

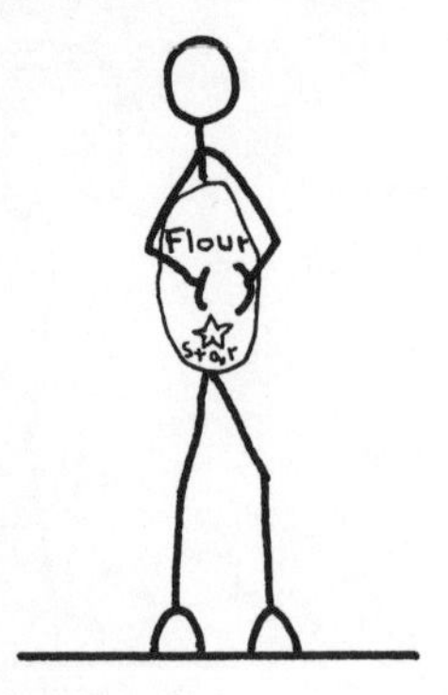

Inefficient
—Hugging the parcel to hold it

Efficient
—Forearms or hands under the parcel

51. GET UNDER IT FOR EFFICIENT CARRYING

4. Get your hands as close to shoulder height as possible. In this position each arm can carry 55 per cent more than when the load is down in front of you. Waiters carry loaded trays at this height, with only one hand, although the tray may be loaded so heavily that he has to crouch down to place it on the tray stand. Efficiently designed restaurant kitchens have a loading rack about breast high on which the waiter places the tray to load it. To carry it, he merely raises one hand close to his shoulder, palm up, bends his knees slightly so he can slip his hand under the middle of the tray, then he straightens up and walks away—nothing to it, not even a grunt needed.

5. When the size and shape of the load permits, carry it close to the elbow joint. When carrying a loaded market basket, for example, it will be easier if the forearm is slipped under the handle so the handle lies in the crotch of the elbow. No hands needed. The power (strength) is greatest when the load is carried near the joint.

6. The most efficient weight to carry is one that is about 30 per cent of your body weight—if you are not overweight. The overweight person is already carrying some extra dead weight every time he moves.

Inefficient

Efficient

52. CARRY CLOSE TO THE BODY WITH ELBOWS CLOSE TO SIDES

Inefficient
—pulling
—feet too far away
—bending over
—back and arms do lifting
—elbows at weak angle

Efficient
—pushing
—feet close to wall
—crouching
—leg muscles do lifting
—elbows at strong angle

53. RAISING A STUCK WINDOW EFFICIENTLY

A sedentary person should not try to carry a load that is more than 40 per cent of his body weight. That hardened one hundred and thirty-pound steel-mill laborer was carrying pigs of iron that were 70 per cent of his body weight, but he was far from a sedentary condition. Do-it-yourselfers sometimes try to carry too heavy loads, to their regret. Young men in a spirit of competition also may try too much of a load. Lifting and carrying are beneficial exercises, but ruptured muscles or sprained backs are not smart.

7. If a load is heavier than 30 per cent of your body weight, put it on wheels or a hand truck. Or, if it has to be moved often, put wheels on it. In one railway shop the heavy jacks used for raising cars were equipped with wheels for easier moving.

8. If wheels cannot be used, then get someone to help you but walk out of step with him while carrying. Better to admit it is too heavy than pay the penalty for overstraining yourself. In industrial operations, it often pays to add an extra man to help with the heavy carrying.

9. Or you may be able to reduce the weight to carrying size. A large-scale illustration of this is fertilizer bags which originally contained 100 pounds. Then they were scaled down to 80-pound size, and now the standard size is 50 pounds.

If the original package is too heavy to carry safely, open it and carry the contents in baskets or pails.

III

Taylor's pioneering experiments on *shoveling* led him to conclude that the most efficient load to shovel was 21 pounds, including the weight of the shovel. With some minor changes, that amount has stood the test of time.

If you are sedentary, or not used to shoveling, play safe and load your shovel lightly enough so you can lift it without exertion to speak of—too many white-collar men have needless heart attacks that are brought on by fully-loaded snow shovels.

1. When the loaded shovel does not have to be raised more than three feet, 20 pounds is the most efficient load.

2. When the load has to be raised higher than three feet, the most efficient load is around 16 pounds.

3. The shovel handle should be long enough so that you do not have to stoop too much—save your back.

4. Use your body weight to help push the shovel into the material, don't do it by muscle movement alone. Simply hold the handle

Inefficient
—hands too close together
—feet too close together
—shovel too close
—he will bend back as shovel goes in
—shovel may take too heavy a load at this angle or the load may slide off

Efficient
—hands far apart for leverage on handle
—feet far apart for balance
—handle against hip while pushing
—he will bend at knees and hips as shovel goes in
—shovel will be more uniformly loaded

54. EFFICIENT SHOVELING

firmly against your thigh, then crouch forward and bend your knees so that your weight pushes the shovel in. Your shoulder and arm muscles will last much longer.

If the material offers too much resistance for that, as in digging hard soil, use your foot to convey your body weight to the shovel. Simply stand on the shovel with one foot; keep the knee joint fairly straight so that your body weight rather than muscle action pushes in the blade.

5. Start the lift, which is usually the most tiring part of the cycle, by using your knee as a fulcrum. Push the far end of the handle down slightly to loosen the blade, slip one knee under the handle toward the load, then pry downward on the far end of the handle while lifting with the hand that is nearer the blade. The load is on its way easily, but will likely need some steering and additional power to get there.

6. If the load has to be thrown some distance, take a few steps in that direction so that a less forceful throw will get the load there. Your legs can take it better than arms and shoulders. Or rearrange the work so that long throws are not needed and save your legs also.

7. When the load has to be thrown to one side, do not twist your back. Instead, change the position of your feet before throwing so the twist can be eliminated. Better yet, rearrange the work.

8. Take it in a steady, rhythmic pace until time to rest, which comes in the following chapter. And if you are sedentary, avoid spurts.

9. And also, anticipating the next chapter, relax the shoveling muscles while they are on the way for another load. Shovel in what the musician would call 4-4 time, this way: PUSH—lift—*throw*—relax on the way back. PUSH—lift—*throw*—relax on the way back, to give a steady rhythm with relaxing included.

20. How to Rest for Efficient Muscle Work

I

WHY CAN'T WE TRUST OUR IMPULSES TO TELL US WHEN TO REST?

While using the vacuum cleaner some housewives cannot resist the impulse to rest after ten minutes of cleaning. Then they take a coffee break, or telephone a friend for a nice long visit, or simply sit and feel sorry for themselves while waiting for their "strength to come back."

Of course they had not lost any strength. The impulse to rest came from disliking the task, not because muscles needed a rest. Studies at Michigan State University have also shown that the women who are the first to feel like taking a rest are the ones who usually do the poorest cleaning job—weak will for that work.

The same misleading impulse is felt by some office and factory workers who do light muscle work which they dislike or find boring. They want to rest long before it is needed, they rest longer than is efficient, and they are usually inclined toward slipshod workmanship.

In contrast, some housewives and workers do like what they have to do and keep plugging hard until the task is finished. These tend to ignore any impulse to rest until it is so strong they cannot deny it. A strong will-to-work.

Those two extremes illustrate how our spontaneous impulses to rest cannot always be trusted. They may prompt us to underwork or overwork, and suggest two practical *guides* worth bearing in mind. (a) When doing work you dislike, or find boring, be careful that you do not rest too much to be efficient. (b) When doing work you enjoy, or are eager to complete, take care to rest enough to keep efficient.

II

How can we decide when, how long, and how to rest?

We can get some useful guides from what scientists have found to produce increased output, or better well-being, when doing various kinds of tasks on actual jobs. Both well-being and the amount done need to be considered. It is not efficient if a great amount of work is turned out but in ways that harm one's well-being. This is especially true when work lasts a long time, such as one's regular occupation, or is really heavy work, such as shoveling wet snow. We will report one study that deals with the amount done, and another that deals with well-being, and which suggest further practical guides.

Dr. George H. Miles, of the National Institute of Industrial Psychology, reported an experiment with factory workers who were doing moderately heavy muscle work. The workers had been resting only on impulse, and had been producing an average of sixteen pieces an hour.

The industrial psychologists observed them at work, minute by minute, to find when they first began to act tired. After about twenty-five minutes of work the average began to slow down. On the basis of that, the workers were given a five minute rest after they had worked twenty-five minutes. Apparently that was a good place for a rest pause, because output went up to eighteen pieces an hour, a gain of 12½ per cent.

Would it be more efficient if these workers were given a rest before they started to act tired or slow down? To get an answer the experimenters tried a two-minute rest pause after only ten minutes of work although the workers were still going strong and had no impulse to rest. But by taking rests then their production jumped to twenty-two pieces an hour—37 per cent more than when they had rested only when they had the impulse.

Under both rest systems the workers rested ten minutes an hour.

But they were much more efficient when they rested before a slump had appeared. Many other experiments and business experience confirm this trend which can be summarized as another general *guide:* Take the rest pause before you begin to slow down, or before you begin to do slipshod work.

Rests on impulse

Rests when tired (Work 25 minutes, then rest 5)

Rests *before* tired (Work 10 minutes, then rest 2)

56. SHORT RESTS BEFORE THEY FELT TIRED WERE BETTER
Hourly output at moderately heavy work

(*Data from Dr. George H. Miles*)

III

Some occupations require heavy enough muscle work to affect bodily well-being unless rests are taken systematically and at suitable times. People who do heavy laboring regularly do take many rests. It is the amateurs, eagerly trying to finish some do-it-yourself project, who neglect the rests. Experienced laborers on highway construction, for instance, obey their impulses to rest an average of twelve minutes each hour. But they do not always take the rests at the best times for their well-being.

The advantage of scheduled rests over impulsive rests is shown by many reports. We will describe one by Dr. Lucien A. Brouha who studied men working in a smelter.

They were doing heavy muscle work, and the smelter was hot; a combination of stresses that could affect well-being. The men did not have to work every minute, fortunately. There was considerable time when they could rest, yet they followed no schedule of rest periods, and sometimes forgot to rest.

When Dr. Brouha examined them at the end of a workday under their own spontaneous rests he found that their body temperatures

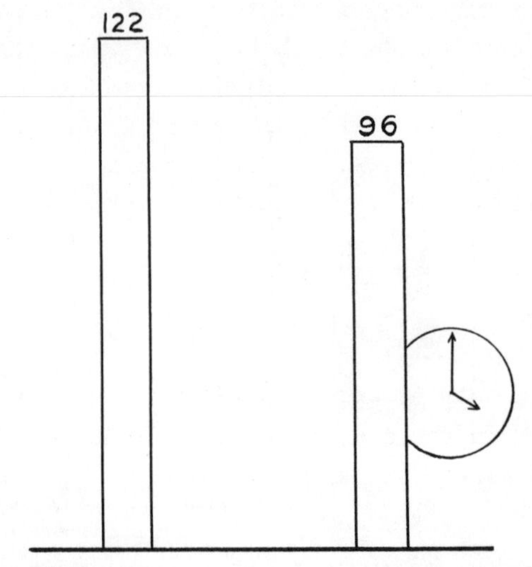

57. SCHEDULED RESTS HELPED THEIR WELL-BEING

Pulse rates of men right after eight hours of heavy work in a smelter (*Data from Dr. Lucien A. Brouha*)

had risen to an average of 99.5 degrees F. Their pulse rates were 122 beats per minute three minutes after quitting work in the afternoon; 110 beats is considered the safe limit.

With such facts as a guide, a schedule for definite rest periods was set up for the men to follow. After those scheduled rests were followed the men were in much better physiological condition at the end of the day. Body temperature averaged a full degree lower than when the rests were not on a systematic basis. And their pulse rate three minutes after stopping work was now down to 96 beats a minute in comparison with the former 122.

Dr. Brouha's observations provide another *guide* for us: Rest at regular periods—"by the clock," not impulse—when you are doing medium or hard muscle work. This is a useful variety of clock watching.

IV

How long should you rest before resuming the muscle work?

If you rest early in the work—before you have slowed down—the rest should be proportionately much shorter. That may seem obvious, but there is more to it than is obvious. Experiments have shown, for instance, that after lifting a weight thirty times it takes four times as long to recover as it does after fifteen lifts. Roughly, this indicates that if you work twice as long your muscles require, not twice as much, but four times as much rest. If you try to work like a superman, you will need a super rest.

How rapidly you have been moving the muscles has a similar unexpected effect. Lift a 13-pound weight as rapidly as you can by one finger, and after about thirty lifts you will be unable to lift it again until you have rested the muscles a half-hour. Working at that furious pace, you could lift it only 120 times during an eight-hour day. But lift it only once every eleven seconds, and you can lift it all day long—2,400 lifts. The slower pace is vastly more efficient because it allows about a ten-second rest pause after about a second of active work; this slow, rhythmic method comes close to "tireless working."

People who are experienced in working with their muscles have often learned to use a pace, or rhythm, which allows a brief rest pause between exertions so they can keep going all day. The amateur starts at a furious pace and is soon so worn down that he is not efficient for the remainder of the day. The few seconds' pause between exertions can be made even more beneficial if the working muscles are intentionally relaxed during the pause.

Some more *guides* are now in order. (a) Use your muscles with a rhythm which allows for a momentary pause between exertions when the task requires repeated use of the same muscles. (b) Take several short rests each hour in preference to a long rest that uses the same total time. (c) As the workday goes on, the rest pauses should usually be made a little longer, particularly when the work is strenuous.

V

Why are short rests preferable?

Probably because there is more recovery during the first part than the second part of a longer pause. One demonstration of this was the rate of recovery after lifting those weights. During the first five minutes' rest 72 per cent of the power to lift the weights was recovered. The next five minutes only 3 per cent more was recovered, and in the next ten minutes only 2 per cent more. In other words, the first five minutes of rest restored fourteen times as much as the next fifteen minutes. That is greatly diminishing returns from longer rest.

Another demonstration came from studies reported by Dr. Arthur G. Bills from the University of Cincinnati on the waxing and waning of the will-to-work during rest pauses. You recall these brought out that there was a steady rise in "readiness to get back to work" during the first seven minutes of the rest pause. From then on, however, their will-to-work took a nose dive and after seventeen minutes' rest there was reluctance rather than readiness to go back to work.

Thus, although a rest pause is usually a good thing, it is an instance where there can be too much of a good thing. A *guide* based on this: Get back to work while your will-to-work is on the rise and before you begin to cool off or lose interest in finishing the job; obey the "impulse to work" before it is replaced by an impulse to rest a bit longer.

VI

Should one lie down during the rest pause from muscular work?

The manager of one of the first factories to use rest pauses installed cots for workers to lie on during the pauses. Strange as it may seem, that is the poorest way to spend the rest period. This is because recuperation depends primarily on the circulation of blood to the muscles that have been worked. To have adequate circulation requires (a) fresh arterial blood being brought to the muscles, and (b) the venous —or "stagnant"—blood being removed from the muscles. Some important practical rest-pause techniques stem from those two requirements.

The fresh supply of blood depends upon the force and speed of the heart, and also upon the size of the capillaries in the muscle. Capillaries dilate in a muscle when it works, permitting more blood flow. But each time the muscle contracts the vessels are compressed by the pressure of the firm muscle, slowing the blood flow. Literally, a tensed muscle strangles itself. That is why a rhythmic work pace, with a brief period of relaxing in the phase of action where least strength is required, is most efficient for such repeated work as hammering, shoveling, etc. During the relaxed part of the rhythm there is a momentary surge of blood to the muscle.

Relaxing for more than a minute or two, however, is not helpful when resting from hard muscle work because of the way venous blood accumulates. The heart pumps blood to muscles but does not suck venous blood back. The venous blood is pumped back by muscles contracting so that veins are squeezed, or "milked," and the stagnant blood is thus moved back toward the heart. This is not a very good system for returning blood, and as a result conditions can quickly become stagnant in a muscle.

That is why people such as barbers and dentists, who stand all day at work, are likely to be bothered by swollen feet and legs. Some barbers wear a larger pair of shoes in the afternoon, or cut slits in their work shoes to allow for their feet to swell after a couple hours of standing. Truck drivers and typists often have similar problems but on a smaller scale. This swelling is the result of venous blood accumulating rather than being milked back toward the heart.

During the rest period it is highly desirable to move the muscles that have been worked, and also the muscles of the feet and lower legs, to milk them of stagnant blood. To refresh the arms after hammering, for instance, move them around, though not vigorously.

Never work so long that you are unable to move at the start of your rest. Don't lie down, and don't sit down for the entire rest period, because moderate general body movement helps muscles recover more rapidly. As a general *guide,* combine relaxing and moving around during the rest period; relax a half-minute, then move around a half-minute.

VII

Should "quick-energy" foods be eaten during the rest pause?

Yes, if you want to put on weight, or if you are going to do really heavy muscle work all day long.

In the chapter "How Hard Is It Safe To Work" we learned that glycogen (blood sugar) is the fuel muscles use, that the glycogen is broken down into lactates, but that about four-fifths of the lactates are synthesized right back into glycogen which can be used again. The muscle-energy supply keeps restoring or rewinding itself in that way so that a little original glycogen can last a long time, provided there are suitable rest pauses for the rewinding to catch up.

Such rewinding of the energy source accounts for the fact that all the muscles of the adult body contain only five to ten ounces of glycogen altogether. There is more stored in the liver, however, to call on if it is needed, which it seldom is. Dr. Bruno Balke found that when sedentary men were given a ten-week period of physical training to get them out of their sedentary condition, their glycogen reserve was increased by 50 per cent.

The glycogen that a sedentary person has on tap is barely scratched by office work and most light factory work. Work up to the optimum level—easy stair climbing, shoveling a 9-pound load, bicycle riding nine miles per hour on the level, walking up a 10 per cent grade—can be done without needing any quick-energy foods between meals.

Those pig-iron carriers, however, were doing maximal work, and did need energy snacks after about two hours of their kind of work. The sandwiches or fruit they ate from their lunchboxes at the rest pauses provided muscle fuel within less than an hour after eating the snack. In those rare instances where energy foods are needed during the work period experiments have shown it is best to take a few nibbles about every half-hour, starting a couple of hours after the work is begun.

There is only one condition under which white-collar workers may profit from a snack at the rest pause. Dr. Waid W. Tuttle directed a series of tests at the University of Iowa on the influence of breakfasts on working efficiency. These showed that a big breakfast was no better in this respect than a medium breakfast; that a bacon-and-eggs breakfast was no better than a cereal breakfast, but that no breakfast lowered working efficiency. When those who had had no breakfast took a snack at the rest pause, their efficiency perked up. But those who had had even a light breakfast were not helped by the rest-pause snack. Coffee during the rest pause helps; food doesn't.

It's smart to mix the right kind of rest, at the right time, and for short times, in with manual work, and to mix relaxing and moving during the pause so that you can have an efficient day with a happy ending.

21. Rest Pauses for White-Collar and Light Work

I

WHY ARE REST PAUSES USUALLY NEEDED FOR SEDENTARY OR LIGHT work?

Such work never depletes the body's energy supply and seldom impairs muscle strength. Yet suitable rest pauses almost always improve efficiency and productivity. We will summarize six conditions under which rest pauses are likely to be most needed and most beneficial.

1. Work that requires *sustained attention,* or is *painstaking,* comes at the top of the list. Watching a radar screen by the hour is a prime example; "mental work," such as serious study, and close handwork, as with fine sewing, should also be included.

After doing this type of work for about fifteen minutes you begin to have periods when the mind "goes blank," or attention is blocked, for a few moments. These blockings are more marked when sleep was short or poor the previous night, or when you feel tired for some other reasons. Occasionally a person worries about these blockings, under the misapprehension that they indicate he is losing control of his thoughts. The only worry about them, however, should be because they lower efficiency for the time being. They are not abnormal.

The blockings become worse and have more effect on output and accuracy as you keep on with the work without resting. You can overcome them a little by tensing muscles and trying hard to give attention to the details. But the best way to overcome them is to take a brief pause.

The ideal time for the pause is just before the blockings begin to interfere, and this time has to be learned by experience. This is another example of the desirabiliy of scheduling regular pauses rather than taking a pause when you happen to feel like it.

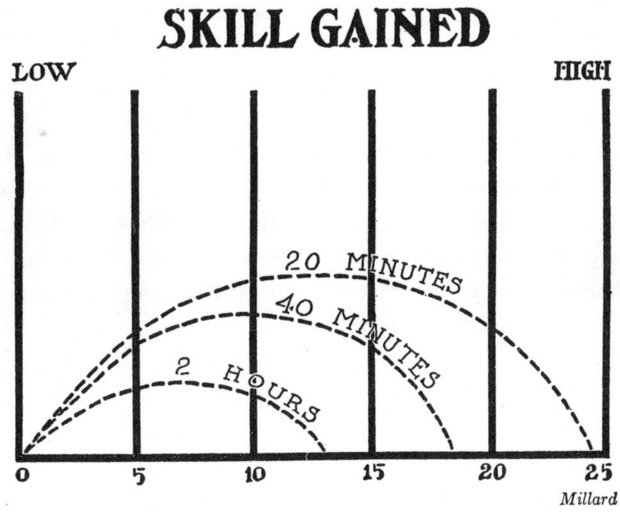

58. Most skill was gained in using a code when they practiced twenty minutes at a time for six times, next most when they practiced forty minutes at a time for three times, least when it was a two-hour work period. The total work was the same in each case, but with six pauses they gained twice as much skill as when no pauses were taken. (From experiments by Dr. Daniel Starch)

2. When the *work is not familiar,* or *taxes your abilities,* blockings become prominent and call for more frequent pauses than with other kinds of work.

Thus the person who is learning a new job needs more, and perhaps longer, rest pauses than he will need after mastering the routines. Job skills are usually acquired faster, too, when practice is broken by rests. Job trainers have recognized for some time that most skills are developed most efficiently when practice periods are short. The chart illustrates one test in which twice as much skill was developed during six practice periods of twenty minutes each than during two hours of continuous practice, although the total time spent in practice was the same.

The person whose abilities are taxed by his work is helped more than the skillful worker by rest pauses. And the slowest workers are almost always benefited more than the fastest workers. In one factory where the girls were pasting labels on bottles, the one-third who were fastest increased their output 8 per cent when rest pauses were adopted, while the one-third who were slowest increased by 17 per cent. Presumably the work is harder for the less skilled (slower), who have to put more effort into the work and hence profit more from the pauses.

3. Work that is *repetitive* and has so much sameness that it gives rise to *monotony* also increases the need for rest pauses. The rest breaks the monotony, and in addition gives the muscles a recuperation period. Although the muscle work may be light, as with folding handkerchiefs, it is usually repeated so continuously on production jobs that the muscles used in the work need a rest. You recall that in handkerchief folding the output was doubled when frequent short rests were used.

4. Work that *does not interest* the person, or *seems meaningless* to him to the point of *boredom,* also calls for rests to relieve the "fed-up" feeling. In these instances the crux of the problem is lack of motivation, or a declining will-to-work. When this is the case some socialization and friendly talk during the pause are believed useful for reviving the will-to-work.

5. Work that is *sedentary,* or which is done in a *constrained posture,* calls for rest pauses in which the sluggish circulation in some parts of the body can be pepped up. The sluggishness is chiefly in the veins because muscles are not moved enough to help milk the blood back toward the heart. Most desk workers have this predicament, as occasional numb legs or swollen feet testify. It is essential to move around during rests when venous sluggishness is a factor.

6. When *muscles are tensed* on the job, rest pauses are essential. We recall that typists get tired necks and sore shoulders because they hold those nonworking muscles tense. Tensed muscles are more frequent then is ordinarily realized on light jobs. The tenseness in muscles that are not used for the work usually occurs when the work is

painstaking, requires sustained attention, or taxes one's abilities. Tensed muscles impede the flow of fresh arterial blood through them because the tenseness squeezes the capillaries. The rest pause gives these muscles a chance to relax, and the instant they do relax there is a surge of fresh blood through them.

II

How should rest pauses be spent by white-collar or light assembly workers?

1. As with rest pauses for heavy work, several short rests are better than one long rest. During the second half of the workday slightly longer pauses may be called for.

2. Moving around and general muscular activity are invariably helpful, largely from their effects in aiding circulation. Walk, swing the arms, do some setting-up exercises. Rest the eyes by looking into the distance; move the eyes in big circles. No need to stand on your head, as one office showoff did.

3. Drink coffee, tea, or a cola drink if you wish. These contain stimulants which make the blockings less noticeable. They are quick acting, the peak stimulation occurring about twenty minutes after drinking and lasting about two and one-half hours. Contrary to common belief, two cups are not twice as stimulating. Also, if you drink a second cup before the stimulation from the first has worn off, there is very little "lift" from the second cup. Drink these about three hours apart, not at every rest pause, to increase efficiency.

4. Do not eat anything, unless you had no breakfast, in which case eat something at the first rest break.

5. Socialize—visit, gossip, laugh—especially if the work is monotonous or boring to you. The monotony or boredom on many jobs is made worse when the work is paced by a conveyor so that there can be no social give and take with other workers. When the pause is spent socializing, it is possible for some of this interest to spill over to the work itself, but do not expect a miracle if you strongly dislike the work.

6. The rest pauses should be scheduled for definite times, or after a certain amount of work has been accomplished. Knowing that a pause is coming gives "something to look forward to," and also pro-

duces a goal gradient spurt. When workers know that a break is coming shortly, they usually increase output before the break—the "home-stretch effect." In one case where office workers added figures all day their output increased 16 per cent just before the pause, and 22 per cent after the pause. An unexpected rest pause may be an appreciated surprise, but it does not have the efficiency value of knowing in advance that one is coming.

III

With light work which does not deplete the bodily resources it is sometimes possible to use *partial substitutes for rest pauses.* These

59. CHANGE WORKING POSITION FREQUENTLY TO IMPROVE EFFICIENCY
Arrange work so it can be done either sitting down or standing up

substitutes cannot always be used in some production jobs that are simplified and repetitive. In designing jobs it would be wise to do everything possible to arrange the work so that these substitutes can be introduced if the need arises, and it almost always does arise.

Some of the substitutes should also be taught during job training, since they require the worker to use his own initiative.

1. Change posture or working position frequently, primarily to help circulation but partly to break any monotony. Most jobs can be arranged so that a worker can either stand or sit. Gilbreth urged "a chair for every job." Students can stand a few minutes while doing home study. A slight change in working posture can often be helpful,

if it is only straightening a leg under the desk or sitting more erectly. Further examples in a moment.

2. Pep up the circulation by occasionally tensing the lower leg muscles to "milk" them and speed the return of venous blood. This is especially needed when work requires mostly standing. It is not needed for walking work because the walking milks the lower veins. Desk workers, however, should tense their legs many times a day and swing their arms and stretch their trunks to get their circulation out of its usual stagnant condition.

Occasional deep breathing—only four or five breaths—helps move venous blood from the abdominal pool where it accumulates in great quantities. Tensing the walls of the lower abdomen also helps. So does a girdle!

3. Work relaxed. (a) Intentionally relax muscles that are not needed for the work, except for the times they are "milked." Keep only enough tenseness to hold an alert posture which will help overcome the blockings of attention. (b) In addition, the muscles being used for the work can usually be relaxed momentarily at some point in the motion cycle; when signing vouchers, relax for an eye wink after each signature, for example.

4. Change your work tempo from time to time. Sometimes a spurt, sometimes a slowdown, but mostly a good steady rhythm. Speed up your reading at the easy parts, slow down and give attention to get the meaning at the harder parts.

When music is used at work, a period of peppy two-steps and marches is usually followed by some slower music to suggest a change of pace. Such changes in work pace are probably most useful when the work is repetitive and on the monotonous side.

5. Switch to different work after spending a half-hour to an hour at one kind. This not only prevents the feeling of sameness, but also gives some of the muscles and brain centers a respite. The housewife can get a semi-rest pause if after a half-hour of vacuum cleaning she sits down and darns socks for fifteen minutes. When planning your work, keep some very different kinds on hand to sandwich in as substitutes for rest pauses.

Most efficiency is gained if the switch is to a much different kind of work. But Victor Herbert applied switching successfully by composing four different operettas at once, switching from one to the other as a substitute for resting. Students can change to a very different subject of study about every hour.

In factories and offices it is often easy to switch work when workers are in teams. In one factory a two-girl team weighed and wrapped the product, with one girl weighing all day, the other wrapping all day. When they swapped jobs twice in the forenoon and twice again in the afternoon, output went up 14 per cent. In a laundry the girl who fed the mangle stood, while her teammate who received the ironed goods sat. When they swapped jobs every twelve minutes their output rose 30 per cent. This had the added advantage of a considerable change of working posture.

Switching to different work has its limitations, especially when the work is heavy. This is illustrated by the joking comments the old-timers often make to young greenhorns who are put to work moving sand in wheelbarrows on construction jobs: "Your job is one long rest. When you're shoveling a load on, you're resting from wheeling. When you're wheeling, you're resting from loading. And when you come back with the barrow empty, you're resting from pushing a load. See? Just one long rest."

6. Add some variety to the work. This is a relative of switching to different work, and is especially useful when the work is monotonous or boring. A few jobs have almost too much variety for one person to handle. The executive often has too many details unless he delegates some. (See our book *The Techniques of Delegating.*) The average private secretary has 132 different duties, and some have more than 400. The housewife and the self-employed individual also usually have more than enough variety.

But in business and industry many jobs are so simplified and specialized that the worker has little variety. In one automobile assembly line, for instance, one-third of the men did only one operation, and it took them two minutes. Another one-third did only from two to five operations as the car passed their work station on the conveyor line. Some of the foremen added some variety to the men's work by asking them to be on the lookout for defects in the paint and upholstery as the cars passed their work stations.

Little additions of that sort can become a semi-rest pause. This was the case with girls who were doing the unskilled, repetitive work of packing eggs in large cases. When they were asked to keep a record of the names of the farmers whose eggs they had packed, that little extra variety gave them a thirty-second semi-rest as they paused to write the name and also perked up their interest in the otherwise monotonous work.

There are usually some ways to make a job more interesting, more challenging, more meaningful, and more satisfying to the individual. The individual, as well as the employer, should try seriously to enrich work in those directions so that the will-to-work becomes stronger than the impulse to rest.

Even when the will-to-work presents no problems, it is still a gilt-edged investment to have rest pauses of the right lengths, at the right times, and spent in the right ways.

22. When You Have to Work Harder Than Usual

I

WE HAVE AN AMAZING CAPACITY FOR DOING HEAVY WORK, PROVIDED we have lived and worked so that our potentials have been developed. As life is lived at present, however, authorities on human biodynamics believe that three out of four adults are so far below what they could be that strenuous exertion for more than a few minutes is hazardous for them. Strenuous exertion can produce severe damage because it greatly increases the demands upon the body, from the marrow inside the bones to the sweat glands on the skin.

Most of us have a pressing need to know how to do heavier work safely, and to have sufficient self-control to work as we know we should and not try to be weekend supermen.

For illustration, we will give figures for a man who is in the prime of life, weighs about one hundred and sixty pounds, and who has developed his working capacities to just a fair degree of efficiency. He is in better working condition than three people out of four, but not in "the pink of condition" of an athlete or hardened laborer. He is in no better condition, however, than most of us could be if we overcame our sedentary handicaps. And the only way to get out of a sedentary rut is to do harder work than usual—in safe ways and in safe amounts that will not injure our well-being.

We will see what happens inside this man, from marrow to sweat glands, as he does everyday work of three intensities:

Exhausting—Shoveling wet snow
Optimal—Easy stair climbing
Mild—A desk job

The bodily processes make remarkable adjustments as they keep up with the changing demands placed on them. The demands that heavy work makes can usually, but not always, be satisfied if the body is given a fair chance. This leads to an important general *guide:* Before starting any work that is more strenuous than you have been used to, plan ways to do it and rest periods that will take advantage of, rather than strain, your bodily adjustments.

II

What is the basic need when we do heavier work?

It is always for more oxygen at the muscles being used the hardest. More oxygen is needed almost instantly. For the three intensities of work the oxygen need by our one hundred sixty-pound man lines up as follows:

Desk work	700	cc. oxygen	per	minute
Easy stair climbing	2,000	"	"	"
Shoveling wet snow	3,000	"	"	"

The amount of oxygen needed is slightly larger for a person who has been sedentary. Whether sedentary or not, the oxygen is needed almost the instant the exertion is increased—by the time you are on the second or third step in climbing the stairs. Fortunately, the supply is increased almost immediately if conditions are favorable for the bodily adjustments to be made.

Although the sedentary person may need as much as 10 per cent more increase in oxygen, it is not increased so quickly nor so adequately for him as it is for those who have kept themselves in good condition for doing heavy work. One everyday consequence of this is shown on the chart of walking up a grade. It was work for 5 per cent of the men to walk up a grade no steeper than the aisle in many church and theater auditoriums. More than half of the men were stopped by a 15 per cent grade. But two men—well-trained athletes —did not reach their crest load until they were going up a 28 per cent grade!

III

How can we make bodily conditions favorable for getting more oxygen?

It's the red cells in the blood that distribute oxygen throughout the body. Whenever heavier work is started, the distribution is speeded

HOW 528 MEN DIFFERED IN CAPACITY FOR WALKING UPGRADE

They stopped when their crest work load was indicated by their pulse reaching 180 beats per minute

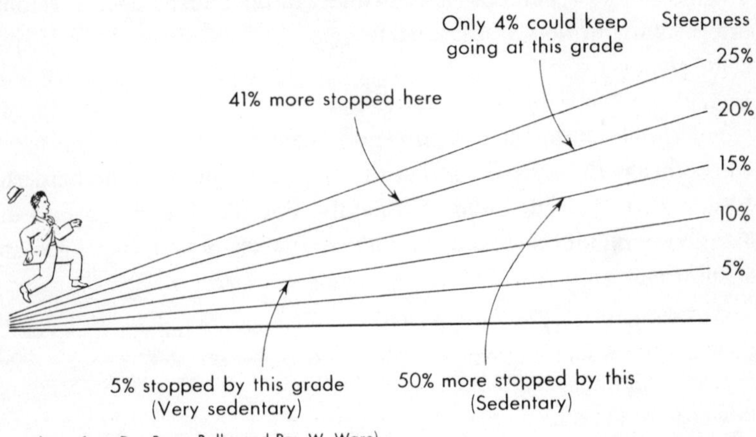

60. HOW 528 MEN DIFFERED IN CAPACITY FOR WALKING UPGRADE

up by the heart pumping more rapidly. As soon as you are on the second or third step your heart is beating 10 to 20 more beats a minute than when you were doing desk work. By the time you reach the top of the stairs, your heart may be beating 140 times a minute.

The more sedentary you are, the more rapidly your heart has to beat when you exert yourself. As the chart shows, very sedentary men's hearts were thumping at 180 beats a minute when they walked up a grade of only 10 per cent steepness. But Olympic athletes could walk up a grade of 28 per cent before their hearts reached that crest load. Shortly we will discover why the athletes' hearts did not have to work so rapidly.

The speeded-up pumping increases the flow of oxygen all over the body, of course. This accounts for the pink skin and flushed face when people do something strenuous. The radiant complexion of your dancing partner, for instance, for social dancing can be strenuous, too.

But the working muscles have a special-delivery system that gives them the lion's share of the speeded-up circulation of red cells. During exertion the blood vessels in the working muscles dilate, providing a larger pipeline; they remain dilated for some time during the rest period.

Another surprising adjustment is that strenuous exercise brings about an increase in the number of red cells in the blood. Ten minutes of hard work may increase the red cells by as much as 10 per cent, giving a definite advantage in getting fresh oxygen where it is needed, and in a hurry. These extra cells are picked up when the blood courses through the dark purple spleen, beside the stomach, where the reserve supply is stored after being manufactured in the bone marrow. This increase in red cells does not last long, unless the exertion continues an hour or two, when it is likely to be a different story which we will come to in a moment.

The person who is used to hard work and the athlete in training have greater oxygen-carrying power than sedentary people. This does not mean that the laborer was born with greater oxygen-carrying power than the man in the office. What happened is that the laborer's daily demands on his bodily processes gradually adjusted them to be able to carry more oxygen. But a week's vacation work (or overwork?) for the man from the office will not make his blood richer in oxygen; it may actually lower his oxygen, for interesting reasons.

In the meantime, this suggests another *guide:* It's smart to take frequent rests when doing harder than usual work so (a) the strain on your heart will be lessened, and (b) the muscles will have a chance to catch up on the oxygen they demand.

IV

Can we help the oxygen supply of the muscles by deep breathing? Fresh oxygen diffuses into the red cells as they pass through the lung tissue. We always need more oxygen than usual in the lungs when doing harder work, and we accomplish this by more frequent and deeper breathing. By the time we are on the second or third step we are breathing a little more rapidly and much more deeply than when we were at desk work, and by the time we reach the top step we may be "out of breath."

Breathing and heart rate work together to supply more-than-usual oxygen, as shown by this summary of what happens in our one hundred and sixty-pound man in the prime of life:

	Heartbeats per minute	*Breaths per minute*	*Air taken into lungs on each breath*
At desk work	98	14	1.2 quarts
At stair climbing	140	18	2.4 "
At snow shoveling	180	30	2.6 "

Note that our man's heart and breathing rates are doubled when he changes from desk work to shoveling snow. And notice especially the amount of air taken in at each breath, which indicates the depth of breathing. There is little difference between stair climbing and snow shoveling in this, for you breathe about as deeply as possible when doing the optimal work of stair climbing. The only way to get more oxygen into the lungs as work becomes harder than that is to breathe more rapidly; the bodily processes see that you do that automatically.

Occasionally a person tries to speed up "getting his breath back" by deliberately taking deeper breaths. Such forced breathing may produce what is called overventilation, which brings on dizziness, numbness, muscle cramps, and mental confusion somewhat similar to some epileptic seizures. Don't force your breathing; let nature take care of it.

After a person has done harder-than-usal work for a few weeks his breathing capacity is usually increased, so that he can take in a pint or two more air than previously on each breath. This is a real advantage. Unfortunately, not every sedentary adult can increase his breathing capacity. There is strong evidence that only those who were active physically in their youth and teen years can increase their lung capacity later in life. Play or work that is strenuous enough to stimulate deep breathing during the growing years seems to enlarge the chest cage, as the bony framework around the lungs is called. When the chest cage is not enlarged by such activity during the growing years, the bones impose a limit on the amount an adult can improve his breathing capacity. As Dr. Peter Karpovich says, "Youth is the time for the development of the chest."

Intentional deep breathing helps return venous blood from the abdominal pool, but it may or may not improve breathing capacity, depending upon how you spent your youth.

Here are some breathing *guides:* 1. While you are working, let nature control your breathing. 2. Rest as soon as you notice breathing is rapid, and before it becomes difficult to breathe; rest until breathing is slow and easy again.

V

Why do I get out of breath so soon in the mountains?

Because you haven't been at the high altitude long enough. Live there a few weeks, and you will be as good as new for doing muscle work.

"Mountain weakness" does not occur in people who live in the mountains. It affects newcomers only—campers and tourists—who are adjusted to lower elevations where the atmospheric pressure is higher. The low pressure at high altitudes slows down the rate at which oxygen diffuses into red cells in the lungs.

Stay at the high altitude for a few weeks, and the bodily processes become acclimatized so that you can work as efficiently as usual. One amazing adjustment is that the number of red cells in the blood increases. Wait until that happens before you try to climb the peak.

A similar problem is presented in airplanes flying at high altitudes. This is solved by having the cabins pressurized, and under some conditions extra oxygen is supplied to the air.

Asthma should be mentioned in this connection, because oxygen is cut down greatly during an attack of the wheezes. Spasms of the muscles around the small air passages in the lungs produce a shortage of oxygen which may become acute during an attack. No need to tell a person to rest from all heavy work during such an attack, because he will rest, if struggling to breathe can be called resting.

Common colds also often interfere with the usual diffusion of oxygen into the red cells. Some allergies cause swelling of the nasal membranes, thus restricting the intake of fresh air into the lungs and causing oxygen shortage.

Carbon monoxide should be mentioned at this point. Some scientists believe this to be a hazard to both health and efficiency, especially in smog-bound cities and under crowded traffic conditions. Carbon monoxide combines with the red cells in such a way as to cut down their oxygen-carrying power permanently. You can become acclimatized to the low pressure of mountain air but not to carbon monoxide.

And although you cannot become acclimatized to allergies, asthma, and colds, you can do much to keep them from lowering your working efficiency if you have skilled medical diagnosis and treatment.

VI

Will I become anemic if I work too hard?

Thousands do on weekends and on their vacations. We learned that there is an increase in red cells during a short bout of hard work. When strenuous work is continued, however, the red cells are used up more rapidly than they can be replaced by reserves from the spleen. This often produces a temporary anemia lasting for a few days.

White-collar workers may have "two-day anemia," on Mondays and Tuesdays: A Saturday superman, a Monday anemic as a result of overwork over the weekend. It may be severe, though brief. After a day of forced marching, for example, seasoned infantry soldiers had a large share of their red cells either destroyed or disintegrated. Their "anemia of work" lasted a couple of weeks, not just Monday and Tuesday.

There are several varieties of anemia that are not caused by overwork, but which impair efficiency by lowering the oxygen-carrying power of the blood. Diet and disease are the common causes. When such an anemic person tries muscle work his face usually becomes pale rather than flushed. It may be pale whether he works or not. He is seldom able to do muscle work except for a brief time.

This brings us to some further *guides:* 1. If you tire quickly, and lack color, you should have a thorough medical examination to find out why. 2. Rest after twenty minutes of more than usually strenuous exercise, whether you are out of breath or not, so (a) you will not destroy red cells, and (b) not use up too much of the reserve in your spleen.

VII

How can I store up oxygen in advance of doing heavier work?

Sorry, but it can't be done. Red cells are stored in the spleen, glycogen is stored in the liver, and both are usually ready to be drawn on as needed. But we have no corresponding storehouse for oxygen which we have to get on a hand-to-mouth basis. After work becomes so heavy—after climbing a couple flights of stairs—we reach a point where muscles need more oxygen than breathing and red cells can supply.

But we do have something almost but not quite as good as a storehouse for oxygen, and this helps us to keep climbing those stairs. This is the muscles' remarkable power to keep on working after they have used up the oxygen immediately available to them—much as if an automobile could keep running after it was out of gas. The muscles do this by "going into debt for oxygen," but this debt always has to be paid off, or else.

This oxygen deficit is a unique feature of muscle chemistry which was discovered largely by Dr. Archibald V. Hill, English physiologist who was awarded a Nobel prize in 1923 for his part in this important discovery.

Here is how your muscles can work after running up an oxygen deficit. The energy-rich glycogen in the muscles goes through a series of transformations which supply energy to support muscle work. Many of the first transformations in the series can be made without needing oxygen. But later in the series oxygen is essential, and if oxygen is not present, the transformations come to a halt. Thus a residue of partially used fuel begins to accumulate. Oxygen is needed sooner or later to complete the transformations in this residue—that is the oxygen deficit.

When a well-trained sprinter runs the 100-yard dash, for example, he piles up an oxygen deficit in ten seconds that takes upward of an hour to pay off. His deeper-than-usual breathing during that hour brings in the oxygen needed to finish the incompleted transformations that accumulated during the ten seconds' all-out exertion.

The same thing happens with the white-collar worker who dashes for the bus. He accumulates an oxygen deficit, too, and his muscles lose strength, become trembly, and may give out before he reaches the bus stop. And it will likely take him much longer than the trained sprinter to make up his deficit. His handwriting may be trembly the first half-hour at the office, and he may resolve to get up a half-hour earlier tomorrow.

An oxygen deficit usually begins to accumulate after a few minutes of heavier-than-usual work. By the time the pulse rate reaches 180 beats a minute the average person's muscles are working mostly on oxygen-deficit transformations.

When the pulse becomes that rapid, the efficiency of the circulation is greatly lowered because there is not enough time between beats for the heart to fill with blood to pump out—the pump loses part of its priming, so to speak. That is one of the reasons why a pulse rate of 180 is looked upon as indicating the crest working load that the body adjustments are able to handle.

A *guide:* Except in serious emergencies, a rest is imperative before the crest load is reached. You can keep on after that point, but it may gravely affect your well-being.

VIII

Is there some way to breathe to pay off the oxygen deficit?

Yes, the way nature makes you. The nerve centers that regulate the rate and depth of breathing will do the job better than you can by trying to breathe differently. The only thing you might do to help nature along is to breathe through your mouth until the distress is past.

Athletes sometimes breathe sniffs of bottled oxygen to speed up paying off the deficit. Football teams may do this between halves. Although this does help, it is not looked upon as good sportsmanship.

What effect habitual smoking has upon paying off the oxygen deficit is unknown.

As good a way as any for paying off the deficit was used by Dr. Charles T. Copeland, one of Harvard's famous teachers. He lived on the third floor of Hollis Hall and students had to climb to his apartment to read their themes aloud to him. Most of the students were out of breath—oxygen deficit—by the time they climbed the long flight of stairs. "Copey" installed a deacon's bench outside the door to his apartment, and students sat there to rest until they got their breath back before knocking on his door.

Guides: 1. Pay off the oxygen deficit by taking it easy and letting nature regulate your breathing. 2. Do some harder-than-usual work—regularly—to develop your capacities to work above sedentary level.

It's always smart to increase one's personal efficiency, in every way possible, from bone marrow to brain cells.

Recommended Readings

Any of these books may be borrowed from a library. If the library does not own a copy, it can borrow one for you on interlibrary loan. Books which were still in print have the 1960 price shown in the listing.

About Taylor:

F. B. Copley: *Frederick W. Taylor.* New York: Harper & Bros., 1923. A two-volume biography.

F. W. Taylor: *Scientific Management.* New York: Harper & Bros., 1947. $6.50. A classic in the field of efficiency.

About the Gilbreths:

Edna Yost: *Frank and Lillian Gilbreth.* New Brunswick, New Jersey: Rutgers University Press, 1949. An easily read biography.

F. B. Gilbreth, Jr., and E. G. Carey: *Cheaper by the Dozen.* New York: Thomas Y. Crowell Co., 1949. $3.50. Two of the Gilbreth children give a hilarious account of their unusual home and family life.

W. R. Spriegel, ed: *The Writings of the Gilbreths.* Homewood, Illinois: R. D. Irwin, Inc., 1956. $9.25. Material from their "secret manual."

About Motion Economy:

R. M. Barnes: *Motion and Time Study.* New York: John Wiley & Sons, Inc., 1958. $9.25. A widely used college text; well illustrated.

R. M. Barnes: *Motion and Time Study Applications.* New York: John Wiley & Sons, Inc., 1958. $3.50. Laboratory problems to accompany the above book.

G. C. Close, Jr.: *Work Improvement.* New York: John Wiley & Sons, Inc., 1960. $7.75. An easily read book intended for foremen. Many examples and pictures. Chapter 11 deals with motion improvement.

L. M. Gilbreth: *Management in the Home.* New York: Dodd, Mead & Co., 1959. $5.00. High-school students could read this book, which is filled with practical examples not only of motion economy in the home but also efficient home management in general.

About Lighting:

W. Allphin: *Primer of Lamps and Lighting.* Philadelphia: Chilton Co., 1959. $10.00. Not very technical, but of more value to the employer than the individual.

W. B. Boast: *Illumination Engineering.* New York: McGraw-Hill Book Co., Inc., 1953. $8.00. Technical text for engineers.

E. W. Commery and C. E. Stephenson: *How to Decorate and Light Your Home.* New York: Coward-McCann, Inc., 1955. $6.75. Well-illustrated book for the general reader.

About Seeing:

H. W. Lyle and T. Keith: *Applied Physiology of the Eye.* Baltimore: Williams & Wilkins Co., 1957. $9.00. Technical presentation.

A. S. MacNalty, ed.: *The Preservation of Eyesight.* Baltimore: Williams & Wilkins Co., 1959. $3.00. A collection of writings by authorities on the subject.

About Climate and Weather:

A. C. Burton and O. G. Edholm: *Man in a Cold Environment.* Baltimore: Williams & Wilkins Co., 1955. $6.75. Technical reports with military significance emphasized.

E. Huntington: *Civilization and Climate.* New Haven: Yale University Press, 1939. $5.50. A classic study which a high-school graduate can read.

E. Huntington and E. B. Shaw: *Principles of Human Geography.* New York: John Wiley & Sons, Inc., 1951. $7.50. A college-level text.

S. F. Markham: *Climate and the Energy of Nations.* London: Oxford University Press, 1944. A scholarly study of the part climate may have played in the rise of nations.

W. F. Petersen: *Man—Weather—Sun.* Springfield, Illinois: C. C. Thomas, Pub., 1947. Studies of the medical effects of climatic conditions.

C. E. A. Winslow and L. P. Harrington: *Temperature and Human Life.* Princeton: Princeton University Press, 1949. $4.00. Another classic study by an authority on ventilation.

About Air Conditioning:

C. H. Burkhardt: *Residential and Commercial Air Conditioning.* New York: McGraw-Hill Book Co., Inc., 1959. $9.00. Technical presentation.

N. C. Harris: *Modern Air Conditioning Practice.* New York: McGraw-Hill Book Co., Inc., 1959. $6.75. Technical presentation.

About Clothes and Foods:

M. D. Erwin: *Clothing for Moderns.* New York: The Macmillan Company, 1957. $5.90. A text for high-school and college students.

L. H. Newburgh, ed.: *Physiology of Heat Regulation and the Science of Clothing.* Philadelphia: W. B. Saunders Co., 1949. Technical reports prepared for the National Research Council.

M. S. Rose, *et al: Foundations of Nutrition.* New York: The Macmillan Company, 1956. $6.25. A textbook.

M. G. Wohl, ed.: *Modern Nutrition in Health and Disease.* Philadelphia: Lea & Fegiber Co., 1960. $18.50. Chapters by authorities, for physicians.

Anon: *Nutritive Values of Foods.* (Home and Garden Bulletin No. 72) Superintendent of Documents, United States Government Printing Office, Washington 25, D.C. 20¢. Reports on some 500 foods.

About Noise:

C. M. Harris, ed.: *Handbook of Noise Control.* New York: McGraw-Hill Book Co., Inc., 1957. $16.50. An authoritative compilation.

About the Will-to-work:

F. Herzberg, *et al: The Motivation to Work.* New York: John Wiley & Sons, Inc., 1959. $4.50. Reports a study of the will-to-work in engineers and accountants. Technical reading, but important.

L. R. Bittel: *What Every Supervisor Should Know.* New York: McGraw-Hill Book Co., Inc., 1959. $7.95. Down to earth, for factory foremen.

D. A. and E. C. Laird: *The Technique of Getting Things Done.* New York: McGraw-Hill Book Co., Inc., 1947. $4.50. Stories of famous people who had a strong will-to-work. For the general reader.

About the Physiology of Work:

W. R. Johnson, ed.: *Science and Medicine of Exercise and Sports.* New York: Harper & Bros., 1960. $12.00. Authoritative reports by specialists. Technical.

P. Karpovich: *Physiology of Muscular Activity.* Philadelphia: W. B. Saunders Co., 1959. $5.50. A textbook for coaches, industrial engineers, teachers of physical education.

Y. Kuno: *Human Perspiration.* Springfield, Illinois: C. C. Thomas, Pub., 1956. $9.50. The most comprehensive research on the topic.

L. E. Morehouse and A. T. Miller: *Physiology of Exercise.* St. Louis: C. V. Mosby Co., 1953. $4.75. Another text for coaches, etc.

L. E. Morehouse and P. J. Pasch: *Scientific Basis of Athletic Training.* Philadelphia: W. B. Saunders Co., 1958. $4.50. For coaches, etc.

D. J. Morton: *Human Locomotion and Body Form.* Baltimore: Williams & Wilkins Co., 1952. $5.00. A scholarly study of walking.

S. Rothman: *Physiology and Biochemistry of Skin.* Chicago: University of Chicago Press, 1954. $19.50. Technical information about perspiring, etc.

About Muscle Dynamics:

M. G. Darrow: *The Posture Problem Up to Date.* New York: Vantage Press, 1959. $3.50. Can be read by high-school graduates.

E. N. Duvall: *Kinesiology—The Anatomy of Motion. Englewood Cliffs,* New Jersey: Prentice-Hall, Inc., 1959. $6.25. A textbook.

B. M. Mensendieck: *Look Better, Feel Better.* New York: Harper & Bros., 1954. $3.50. Easily-read account of methods for improving muscular control and movements.

E. Betheny: *Body Dynamics.* New York: McGraw-Hill Book Co., Inc., 1952. $4.95. A textbook with a good chapter on relaxation; woman's angle emphasized.

About Other Aspects of Personal Efficiency:

J. Brothers: *10 Days to a Successful Memory.* Englewood Cliffs, New Jersey: Prentice-Hall, Inc., 1957. $4.95. A peppy book that is scientifically sound in spite of its title.

E. Jacobson: *You Must Relax.* New York: McGraw-Hill Book Co., Inc., 1957. $4.75. For the general reader, by the originator of progressive relaxation.

R. Josephs: *How to Gain an Extra Hour Every Day.* New York: E. P. Dutton & Co., 1955. $2.95. A popularly written book reporting time-saving tricks used by famous people.

D. A. and E. C. Laird: *The Techniques of Delegating.* New York: McGraw-Hill Book Co., Inc., 1957. $3.95. For the general reader and the executive who get things done through others.

D. A. and E. C. Laird: *Sound Ways to Sound Sleep.* New York: McGraw-Hill Book Co., Inc., 1959. $4.50. An account of current scientific teachings for the general reader.

E. J. McCormick: *Human Engineering.* New York: McGraw-Hill Book Co., Inc., 1957. $8.00. A college textbook describing scientific methods of adjusting jobs to people.

C. T. Morgan and J. Deese: *How to Study.* New York: McGraw-Hill Book Co., Inc., 1957. $1.50. A paper-bound book widely used by students.

N. B. Smith: *Read Faster and Get More from Your Reading.* Englewood Cliffs, New Jersey: Prentice-Hall, Inc., 1958. $5.95. A how-to book.

Index